THE BIBLICAL DOCTRINE OF JUDGMENT

The Biblical Doctrine of Judgment

by
LEON MORRIS, B.Sc., M.Th., Ph.D.
Warden, Tyndale House, Cambridge

Wipf & Stock
PUBLISHERS
Eugene, Oregon

Wipf and Stock Publishers
199 W 8th Ave, Suite 3
Eugene, OR 97401

The Biblical Doctrine of Judgment
By Morris, Leon
Copyright©1960 Inter-Varsity Press, UK
ISBN: 1-59752-817-X
Publication date 7/12/2006
Previously published by The Tyndale Press, 1960

CONTENTS

I JUDGMENT IN THE OLD TESTAMENT: SHAPHAT   7

II JUDGMENT IN THE OLD TESTAMENT: WORDS OTHER THAN
   SHAPHAT   26

III JUDGMENT IN THE NEW TESTAMENT: A PRESENT REALITY   44

IV JUDGMENT IN THE NEW TESTAMENT: A FUTURE CERTAINTY   54

THE TYNDALE
BIBLICAL THEOLOGY LECTURE, 1960

This is an expanded form of the lecture delivered in Cambridge on July 6th, 1960, at a meeting convened by the Tyndale Fellowship for Biblical Research

Unless otherwise stated Scripture quotations
are from the Revised Version.

CHAPTER I

JUDGMENT IN THE OLD TESTAMENT: SHAPHAT

THE basic Old Testament idea about judgment may be summed up very simply in the words of Deuteronomy i. 17, 'the judgement is God's'. This is not to deny that there is much in the Old Testament about the judgment of man as well as about that of God. Indeed, it is probable that, if we could trace the history of the word back to its remotest origins, we should find that its first use was for the judgment that men exercise. Then, when their own practice had given them the concept of judgment, men began to apply it to the mighty acts of God and to think of Him as active in judgment. Even so, we should have to bear in mind that as far as we know judgment was never a purely secular process. From the earliest times it was a religious activity. Moses could say, 'the people come unto me to inquire of God . . . and I judge between a man and his neighbour' (Ex. xviii. 15f.).[1] Judgment was an activity of a 'man of God'.[2]

Whatever be the right order chronologically there can be no doubt that theologically the divine has the place of first importance, at any rate in the developed religion of the Old Testament. Judgment, as the Hebrews came to understand it, is first and foremost an activity of God. Yahweh is 'a God of judgement' (Is. xxx. 18), or even 'the God of judgement' (Mal. ii. 17). Judgment is His own activity, for no-one 'taught him in

[1] W. O. E. Oesterley regards this as giving us the fundamental idea: 'The Hebrew word for to "judge" means originally to pronounce the oracle' and he cites Ex. xviii as evidence (Hastings one-volume *Dictionary of the Bible*, article on 'Judges'). Arnold C. Schultz takes a similar view in *Baker's Dictionary of Theology* (Grand Rapids, 1960).

[2] Cf. C. Ryder Smith, 'it looks as if any man, whom people recognized for any reason to be a "man of God"—whether because he was a prophet like Samuel, or a priest like Eli, or a saviour of his people like Gideon, or merely a man whom Jehovah had evidently prospered, like Abdon—might "judge"' (*What is the Old Testament?* London, 1939, p. 93). The significant thing is the connection with God. Any 'man of God' might judge, but only a 'man of God' might judge.

the path of judgement' (Is. xl. 14). He 'does' judgment and may be relied upon to do it (Gn. xviii. 25).[1] He loves judgment (Is. lxi. 8). Judgment is as natural to Him as the movements of the birds are to them (Je. viii. 7).[2] 'All his ways are judgement' (Dt. xxxii. 4). Judgment (together with righteousness) is 'the foundation of his throne' (Ps. xcvii. 2). In line with this nine times over Yahweh is spoken of as 'Judge'. Abraham calls Him 'the Judge of all the earth' and confidently appeals to Him in this character, 'shall not the Judge of all the earth do right?' (Gn. xviii. 25). In similar strain Jephthah can say, 'the Lord, the Judge, be judge this day between the children of Israel and the children of Ammon' (Jdg. xi. 27). The Psalmist prays boldly, 'Lift up thyself, thou judge of the earth: render to the proud their desert' (Ps. xciv. 2).

Such passages as these leave no doubt but that the Old Testament associates judgment closely with the Lord. It is His function. He engages in judgment and men know that He does so. They can appeal to Him in His capacity as Judge. His judging activity is not confined to Israel. He is 'the Judge of all the earth'. But, as we might expect, it is His activities in connection with His own people that come in for most attention.

I. THE FUNDAMENTAL IDEA: SOME SUGGESTIONS

All this does not tell us exactly what the Hebrews of the Old Testament understood by judging. Granted that it was associated with the Lord, and with the service men should offer Him, what precisely did the Hebrews understand by the term? Scholars cannot be said to have reached even general agreement on this point. Three main lines of approach may be discerned, namely, those which see as the fundamental idea rule, custom, or discrimination. We examine each of these in turn.

1. Judgment and Rule

There is no question but that on occasion 'to judge' and 'to rule' are not far apart, and this so impresses some scholars that they

[1] 'Right' in this verse is *mishpaṭ*, 'judgment'.
[2] *Mishpaṭ* is here translated 'ordinance'. There is no question but that the Lord's *mishpaṭ* is being spoken of.

conclude that 'rule' is the basic idea in *shaphat*, and that the idea of judging is secondary. H. W. Hertzberg[1] and V. Herntrich[2] may be cited as holding this point of view. C. H. Dodd seems to take it as axiomatic.[3] Support is found in passages in the Bible which link the two ideas closely. Thus, when the people wanted Samuel to give them a king, they said, 'make us *a king to judge* us like all the nations' (1 Sa. viii. 5).[4] Again, at the beginning of his reign Solomon prayed, 'Give thy servant ... an understanding heart to judge thy people' (1 Ki. iii. 9; cf. 2 Ch. i. 11, 'that thou mayest judge my people, over whom I have made thee king').

But probably the most important evidence for this view is found in the Book of Judges. The function of the people whose title gives the book its name was not primarily legal. While there is no reason to doubt that these men did on occasion perform functions that we should recognize as judging, their primary function lay elsewhere. More than anything else they were deliverers,[5] men raised up by God to meet special needs, and to deliver their nation in specific times of oppression. As a result of their military successes they became the accepted leaders and rulers of the people. When we are told that such-and-such a man 'judged' Israel this means, to all intents and purposes, that he ruled the nation.[6]

Yet even here the term 'judge' is not exactly synonymous with 'ruler'. Daniel-Rops can define it as 'he who protects by means

[1] See his article 'Die Entwicklung des Begriffes מִשְׁפָּט im AT', *Zeitschrift für die Alttestamentliche Wissenschaft*, xl, pp. 256-287.
[2] *Theologisches Wörterbuch zum Neuen Testament*, vol. iii, p. 922.
[3] He says that κρίνειν means 'to separate, discriminate' and proceeds, 'The Hebrew שָׁפַט, which it is used to translate, has no such associations: it denotes an act of sovereignty, expressed either in legislation or in the administration of justice' (*The Interpretation of the Fourth Gospel*, Cambridge, 1953, pp. 208f.). Besides ignoring much of the evidence about *shaphat* this overlooks the fact that 'rule' includes much more than legislation and the administration of justice.
[4] In verse 20 they thought of being 'like all the nations' and interestingly put 'that our king may judge us' before 'and go out before us, and fight our battles'.
[5] *Moshia'*, 'saviour', is used of judges in Jdg. iii. 9, 15.
[6] This is probably the meaning also of the complaint of the men of Sodom concerning Lot, 'This one fellow came in to sojourn, and he will needs be a judge' (Gn. xix. 9).

of justice'.¹ That is to say, there is a strong flavour of 'right' about the word. It does not denote power naked and unashamed, but power directed towards right ends. The idea of rule is there. There is no question about that. But even when the idea of rule is present and is dominant the idea of justice is present also as a fundamental undertone. The 'judge' is more than simply a ruler. He is one whose activity is fittingly described in terms of law and justice.²

Nor should we overlook the religious aspect. The judges did not choose themselves. Nor did the people choose them. It was the Lord who raised them up (Jdg. ii. 16, 18).³ The divine initiative strengthens our conviction that there is a basic connection with justice, for His actions are thought of as right. Thus when Deborah sang of His triumphs she did not think simply of His power and His might, but of 'the righteous acts of the Lord' (Jdg. v. 11). Yahweh acts in accordance with fundamental right. Those whom He appoints may be expected to do the same.

It is beyond doubt that the judgment word group was applied to legal as well as governmental activity. It is an argument against the primacy of the latter that it is not as easy to see how it could give rise to the idea of judgment as it is to envisage the reverse process. When the dispensing of legal judgment became the established practice it would normally be carried out by the leading men of the community. Under the monarchy the king would be the judge *par excellence*. He would constitute the final

---

¹ *Israel and the Ancient World*, London, 1949, p. 119.

² W. I. Wolverton says that the judge 'adjudicated cases and guaranteed a measure of inner stability in the tribe or sept' (*Ang. Theol. Rev.*, xli, p. 278). The order is important.

³ S. Mowinckel emphasizes this aspect of the judges' activity, and cites Alt and Michelet for the view that their chieftainship was 'charismatic', as dependent on Yahweh's 'grace-gift' (*He that Cometh*, Oxford, 1956, p. 58). He thinks of judging, incidentally, as a comprehensive expression for the varied qualities and activities of the chieftain (*loc. cit.*), and if at times he appears to understand this very much in terms of rule he can define 'to judge' as 'to rule rightly, to do the right thing, and in general to maintain due order in affairs' (*op. cit.*, p. 68). When he comes to deal with kingship he points out that the situation in Israel differed from that in other nations, for there 'the king's essential task is to be the instrument of Yahweh's justice and covenant blessing among men' (*op. cit.*, p. 94). Not rule, but justice (and the justice of Yahweh at that) is primary.

court of appeal. And only he could be called 'the judge of Israel'. Others would judge within a more limited sphere. Moreover, the king could enforce his judicial decisions, which would make him judge in a special way.[1] It is thus not so very difficult to see how the thought of 'rule' could arise from that of 'judge'. But it is not so easy to see how a word meaning 'rule' would come to mean 'judge'. A king does many things, and there is no really good reason why ruling should be equated with one of them, namely, judging.

Also against the idea of rule as prior is the widespread use of the words from the root in the sense of discrimination. They are to be found throughout the Old Testament, whereas the thought of rule is mostly to be found in the book of Judges, and in connection with Solomon (there is only a sprinkling of references to rule elsewhere). Such a distribution is unlikely if rule is prior and judging no more than a derived usage.

2. Judgment and Custom

The second understanding of the root sees the basic idea in custom. Law lends itself to precedent, and precedent to settled custom. Without question the noun *mishpat* is often used in this way. Thus in Psalm cxix. 132 we read, 'have mercy upon me, as thou usest to do (lit. "according to *mishpat*") unto those that love thy name'. At Jericho the Israelites 'compassed the city after the same manner (*mishpat*) seven times' (Jos. vi. 15). There is a *mishpat* 'to every purpose' (Ec. viii. 6). Such *mishpat* is not confined to Israel. The priests of Baal in their contest with Elijah 'cut themselves after their *mishpat* with knives and lances' (1 Ki. xviii. 28). 1 Samuel viii. 11-17 gives a detailed explanation of the *mishpat* against which Samuel warns the people. It is instructive both in itself, and as indicating that Israel was not to follow all *mishpat*. Her *mishpat* was that that flowed from her relation to Yahweh. All other *mishpat* was to be eschewed.

N. Snaith is one who sees in this connection with custom the basic idea of the whole word group. 'The primary idea according

---

[1] This may give the meaning of Jdg. xvii. 6, 'In those days there was no king in Israel: every man did that which was right in his own eyes'. A king was needed to enforce decisions.

to usage is judgement by custom, for the function of a judge is to give decisions according to custom or precedent.'[1] He differentiates *mishpaṭ* from *torah* by saying that the former is a decision where there is a precedent to follow, while the latter is revealed 'by sacrifice or sacred lot if he were a priest, by dream or in ecstasy or vision, if he were a cult prophet'.[2] But Snaith does not carry this idea through to its logical conclusion. He has to say 'no judge, whether priest or prophet, could give any other judgements than those which are regarded as being the veritable word of God'.[3] This concession is all-important. For the men of the Old Testament the connection with God is the primary thing. Custom is important, and there is often no good reason for disturbing the established way of doing things. But the basic thought is that of relationship to Yahweh, not that of conformity to human custom. It is this which invalidates J. Pedersen's contention that Yahweh's will 'was determined by the totality of Israelite customs, *mishpāṭ*, and was expressed in the laws'.[4] This is surely to put the cart before the horse. It is not the nation and its ways that takes the first place in the Old Testament. It is God. The nation's first duty is to obey His commands. *Mishpaṭ* is to be exercised within this framework.

Those who so stress custom ignore the revolutionary dynamic which is characteristic of the religion of the Old Testament, and which finds expression in the 'judgment' concept. In the Bible there is none of the quiet acceptance of the *status quo* so characteristic of the polytheistic religions. G. Ernest Wright has pointed out, for example, that in the Egyptian wisdom literature

---

[1] *The Distinctive Ideas of the Old Testament*, London, 1950, p. 76.

[2] *Op. cit.*, p. 75; *A Theological Word Book of the Bible*, ed. Alan Richardson, London, 1950, p. 117. In neither place does he cite any evidence. J. Pedersen takes a different view when he says that *mishpaṭ* is 'the same as *ḥōḳ* (the established), *tōrā* (instruction), *miṣwā* (tradition)' (*Israel*, I-II, London, 1926, p. 351).

[3] *Distinctive Ideas*, p. 76.

[4] *Israel*, III-IV, London, 1947, p. 160. Cf. also Th. C. Vriezen, 'the original meaning is rather use and wont, custom, especially that which is in keeping with a certain relationship in life and therefore that which is proper' (*An Outline of Old Testament Theology*, Oxford, 1958, p. 327). E. W. Heaton also maintains that 'the words *mishpaṭ* ("judgement") and *tsedeq* ("righteousness") both mean the recognized norm of a group' (*His Servants the Prophets*, London, 1949, p. 82).

the contrast is between the 'passionate man' and the 'silent man'. 'The latter is the successful man because he is always calm and never a disturber of the established order.' The former 'destroys that harmonious integration in the existing order which alone is effective'.[1] A similar situation obtains elsewhere. In the ancient world in general there is a concern to maintain the established order, and this concern is bolstered by official religion.

In Israel, however, the contrast is made between the righteous and the wicked. When the righteous 'does judgment' he does not necessarily preserve the established order. On the contrary, if the wicked are in power he disrupts it with considerable vigour. And what in this way he does partially and imperfectly he constantly looks for Yahweh to accomplish fully and perfectly. It is no coincidence that the men of the Old Testament looked for a 'day of the Lord' when there would be a catastrophic overthrow of the established order and the bringing in of God's perfect order.

Mishpaṭ must also be seen against the background of God's election of His people. The Old Testament knows of other *mishpatim* than its own. But Israel is not to follow the *mishpaṭ* of the heathen. There is no reverence for custom as such. For Israel *mishpaṭ* derives its content from her relationship with Yahweh. She knows *mishpaṭ* only because of what He has revealed. *Mishpaṭ* is a dynamic theological concept, not a way of describing the established order. To take an example at random, when Amos tells Israel that Yahweh says, 'I hate, I despise your feasts, and I will take no delight in your solemn assemblies . . . let judgement roll down as waters, and righteousness as a mighty stream' (Am. v. 21-24), it is impossible to hold that he is urging the retention of the *status quo*. He is advocating radical reform. Far from denoting an adherence to custom, a retention of the old order, *mishpaṭ* is nothing less than revolutionary dynamite.

It should also be pointed out that the view that the root basically means conformity to custom requires that we take the noun *mishpaṭ* as the basic member of the word group. No-one, as far as I know, argues seriously that the verb *shaphaṭ* means 'to conform to custom' or the like. But *mishpaṭ* is obviously a derived

---

[1] *The Old Testament against its Environment*, London, 1950, p. 44. He quotes the words about the 'passionate man' from Frankfort.

word, and not the basic word of the root. There could scarcely be a prefixed form until there was something to which the prefix could be attached.¹ We would need some convincing evidence before accepting a word which has every appearance of being a derivative as the original word in the group.

3. Judging as Discrimination

The third idea is that the fundamental meaning of the word group is that of discrimination, of distinguishing between parties. It is this we see when Moses says, 'I judge between a man and his neighbour' (Ex. xviii. 16), or when he charges the judges, 'Hear the causes between your brethren, and judge righteously between a man and his brother, and the stranger that is with him' (Dt. i. 16). In the same manner Solomon prayed, 'Give thy servant . . . an understanding heart to judge thy people, that I may discern between good and evil' (1 Ki. iii. 9). Passages like these are widespread, and they convince authorities like H. Ferguson,² E. Jacob,³ and L. Köhler⁴ that discrimination is the basic meaning. This view can claim a measure of support also

---

[1] O. Booth has an article on 'The Semantic Development of the term מִשְׁפָּט in the Old Testament' (*Journal of Biblical Literature*, vol. lxi, pp. 105-110). He says many valuable things as he argues that the original meaning is custom. But he totally ignores the existence of the verb *shaphaṭ*. On the form Hertzberg says, 'nouns of the form miqtal denote a state or an act whereby the action in the corresponding verbal stem comes to expression' (*op. cit.*, p. 260). Nouns of this formation sometimes denote place (here it would be 'place where judgment is dispensed'). But this hardly affects the argument other than to underline the derived character of nouns of this type. See also the discussion in Gesenius' *Hebrew Grammar*, ed. E. Kautzsch, revised A. Cowley, Oxford, 1952, 85 *e-m*.

[2] He says, 'The point of the inquiry is whether the idea of ruler is primitive and that of judge derived from it, or *vice versa*. The results of my investigation have convinced me that the idea of judging or deciding questions is the primitive one, and the idea of ruling has been superadded' (*Journal of Biblical Literature*, vol. viii, p. 131).

[3] *Theology of the Old Testament*, London, 1958, p. 96, n. 3. He is following van der Ploeg.

[4] In his lexicon he gives the first meaning of the verb as 'decide, settle a dispute between'. In *Hebrew Man*, London, 1956, p. 157n. he says,: '*Shaphaṭ* originally means "to decide between," *mishpaṭ* means in most cases "a decision which is valid for a person"'. He derives other meanings from this.

from the cognate languages.[1] And it is beyond dispute that the word group came to be used very largely for judicial processes. These, involving as they do a necessary act of discrimination, point in the same direction. It seems to me that this is the way the word group should be understood.

What is this function of judging? How was it exercised? While it is basically a legal process, it is not to be equated with judging in our sense of the term. We understand it of the activity of legal personnel, specially trained for the purpose, who give an impartial verdict on the basis of the evidence brought before them. We take for granted what Edmund Burke called 'the cold neutrality of an impartial judge'. This was not the work of a judge in ancient Israel. We may obtain help in arriving at an understanding of the position by considering the apocryphal book of Susanna.[2] The date of this writing is comparatively late, but the activity of judging it depicts is a faithful reflection of a much more ancient practice.

When Susanna was condemned to death on the evidence of false witness (the sentence being given by 'the assembly', verse 41), proceedings were halted by Daniel. He does not seem to have held any official position. He is described simply as 'a young youth

[1] Thus H. Ferguson points out that where it occurs (it is not found in all the related languages) it refers to the magistrates and their work, as in the Carthaginian *sūfēt* (*op. cit.*, p. 131). V. Herntrich finds the meaning in Assyrian much the same as in Hebrew with a similar variation between the ideas of judgment and rule (*op. cit.*, p. 923). Snaith finds the word group in Akkadian, Phoenician, Aramaic and Punic. He thinks that 'The root has to do with the verdict given by a judge . . . and it is used of every phase of a judge's work, discriminating the truth, Zechariah vii. 9; deciding controversies, vindicating or condemning, and even, in the niphal form, of entering into a controversy to see who is in the right, Isaiah xliii. 26' (*op. cit.*, p. 74). I am indebted to Prof. W. S. LaSor for the information that in Ugaritic the word group expresses the ideas of judging and of ruling, as in Hebrew. There is also a name of the god Yamm, *ṭpṭ nhr*, which Prof. LaSor believes 'goes back to the "trial by ordeal" by which a person suspected of guilt was thrown into the river: if he drowned he was guilty, if not he was innocent'. This ancient name clearly presupposes judicial discrimination. Prof. LaSor finds much Akkadian evidence indecisive, but all the passages he lists from the Mari tablets point to judicial activity, not rule.

[2] See also the excellent treatment of the subject by L. Köhler, *Hebrew Man*, pp. 149-175. He gathers Old Testament passages to show how a legal assembly was convened and how it functioned.

($\pi\alpha\iota\delta\acute{\alpha}\rho\iota o\nu$ $\nu\epsilon\omega\tau\epsilon\rho o s$)' (verse 45). Despite his tender years the assembly gave heed to him and returned to the place of judgment saying, 'Come, sit down among us, and shew it us, seeing God hath given thee the honour of an elder' (verse 50). Daniel proceeds to the examination of the witnesses with no nonsense about judicial impartiality. He addresses the first in these terms: 'O thou that art waxen old in wickedness, now are thy sins come home to thee which thou hast committed aforetime, in pronouncing unjust judgement, and condemning the innocent, and letting the guilty go free' (verses 52f.). When this man has given his evidence Daniel says, 'Right well hast thou lied against thine own head; for even now the angel of God hath received the sentence of God and shall cut thee in two' (verse 55). The second witness is hailed as 'O thou seed of Canaan, and not of Judah, beauty hath deceived thee, and lust hath perverted thine heart' (verse 56). His evidence is followed with 'Right well hast thou also lied against thine own head: for the angel of God waiteth with the sword to cut thee in two, that he may destroy you' (verse 59). The result of Daniel's interrogation is that the false witness is exposed and Susanna vindicated.

This lively story shows us the judge appointing himself, though with the consent of the assembly. He apparently has no special qualifications. He does not wait passively for evidence to be brought before him, but goes out after it. His chief interest is not in the pursuit of some abstract concept of justice, but in delivering the weak from unjust condemnation. That this is not an ethical duty, but a religious activity, is indicated by the conclusion, when the assembly 'cried out with a loud voice, and blessed God, who saveth them that hope in him' (verse 60).

This is judgment as the Hebrews conceived it. There is a basic activity of discrimination.[1] Daniel discriminated between the elders and Susanna, between the words of the elders and the truth of the matter. This activity of discrimination is fundamental to the meaning of *shaphaṭ*.

But judging meant not only a mental activity of weighing evidence, of sifting the false from the true. Judging was essentially

[1] Cf. C. Ryder Smith, 'The meaning of the word is nearly what we mean by "arbitrate"' (*op. cit.*, p. 93).

dynamic. An Israelite could say to Moses, 'Who made thee a prince and a judge over us? thinkest thou to kill me, as thou killedst the Egyptian?' (Ex. ii. 14). Moses' slaying of the Egyptian hardly looks to us like the action of a judge. But it implied a passion for the right, an existential concern that justice be done.[1] The judge not only discovered what was right, but acted on it. If all the evidence was not in he went out until he found what was missing, that justice, real justice, be done. Thus one and the same verb may mean 'to punish' or 'to deliver'.[2] Jehu's extermination of the house of Ahab is described as 'executing judgement upon the house of Ahab' (2 Ch. xxii. 8), while the godly can pray, 'O Lord, thou hast seen my wrong; judge thou my cause' (La. iii. 59). 'Judge' and 'judgement' are frequent in both senses in the Old Testament.

II. JUDGMENT AND ACTION

It must be emphasized that, whether the judgment be that of the Lord or that of men, it is fundamentally dynamic. Basically judgment is the process whereby one discerns between the right and the wrong *and takes action as a result*. There is dispute between two, a determination as to the rights of the matter, and then— action. The dynamic character of the word must be stressed. It is not an intellectual activity carried out in academic detachment. It is not an exercise in balancing evidence. It is an activity of discrimination and vindication. He who does *mishpat* seeks out the wrongdoer to punish him, and the righteous to vindicate his cause.

Judgment is not confined to legal matters. Indeed, we could go so far as to say that the really significant use of judgment begins when it is separated from all legal and governmental functions and applied to conduct in general. Judgment is a quality of

---

[1] It also implied a claim to supremacy, so that Moses might be described as 'prince' as well as 'judge'.

[2] Cf. E. Jacob, 'The outcome of the judgment is a veritable liberation for the one who has been the object of a declaration of innocence, since he is not only reinstated in his right, but by the operation of the power of which he has been a beneficiary his life-potential is in some way augmented; the *mishpat* of the judge "establishes the one in the reality of his right, the other on the contrary in the reality of his wrong"' (*op. cit.*, p. 97; the last words are cited from A. Neher).

action. Again and again men are urged to 'do judgment and justice', to 'judge justly' and the like. These are not exhortations to enter the legal profession. They are ways of driving home the truth that, in their ordinary lives day by day, men must exercise the quality of judgment, of discrimination. This does not mean simply that they are to discern right from wrong. They are to do that, but to 'do judgment' means that they will also actively pursue the right. *Mishpaṭ* denotes a dynamic 'right-doing'. This is not right action in general, but specifically right action as the result of discrimination. There is always the fundamental thought of distinguishing between the right and the wrong. But there is always also the added thought of decisive action as the result of that discrimination.

Especially is this to be seen in helping the weak, the poor, the defenceless. Judgment has a salvation aspect.[1] 'Learn to do well; seek judgement, relieve the oppressed, judge the fatherless, plead for the widow' (Is. i. 17). Passages like these lead Köhler to say 'in Hebrew, "to judge" and "to help" are parallel ideas'.[2] Zechariah gives the duty of man in these words, 'These are the things that ye shall do; Speak ye every man the truth with his neighbour; judge truth and the judgement of peace in your gates: and let none of you imagine evil in your hearts against his neighbour; and love no false oath' (Zc. viii. 16, RV mg.). Micah's famous summary also includes judgment: 'He hath

[1] Cf. the use of *moshiaʻ*, 'saviour', of judges noted above. W. I. Wolverton maintains that the judgment words 'in the earlier period of Israel's history refer to an aspect of rule in which the public authority, be he chief, nobleman or king, acted in a saving or delivering manner to those in distress' (*op. cit.*, p. 285). I do not think that rule is the primary idea, but Wolverton's emphasis on the humaneness that is integral to this word group is important. S. Mowinckel also draws attention to this aspect of the word group, saying of the Messiah, 'his task in the future kingdom is to "judge" Yahweh's people. That means defending them from any attack or encroachment, driving the enemy back when he ventures forth, and ruling the land with justice and righteousness for the good fortune and success of the people' (*op. cit.*, p. 178).

[2] *Op. cit.*, p. 156. He also says, 'This correct statement of the linguistic evidence explains why the characters who free the Israelite tribes and groups of tribes from foreign domination in the period before the monarchy are called "judges". They are not men who pronounce judgment, but "helpers", war being here regarded as the means by which right is achieved' (*op. cit.*, p. 157).

shewed thee, O man, what is good; and what doth the Lord require of thee, but to do justly (lit. "do judgment"), and to love mercy, and to walk humbly with thy God?' (Mi. vi. 8).

Such passages regard the doing of judgment as one of the basic requirements laid by Yahweh on His people. And He lays this requirement on His people because He is essentially just, just in His inner being.[1] Justice is not a matter indifferent, but one of passionate concern. Because judgment matters so intensely to Yahweh it is integral to the religious life of those who call themselves by His name. The man who does judgment has a due regard for law, not for law in general, not for some abstract concept of ethical uprightness, but for the law of Yahweh. Judgment represents the discharge of his obligation to Yahweh. This necessarily takes place within the covenant community, and thus it is closely linked with the whole idea of covenant. Indeed, G. Pidoux maintains that in the Bible 'to judge is inseparable from the concept of the covenant. When two persons enter into a covenant they have rights and duties with respect to each other. They are *just* in so far as they observe the obligations imposed by the covenant. To judge is, above all, to act in such a way as to maintain the covenant.'[2] The individual Israelite was bound to God and to other Israelites by the covenant tie. Judgment must be exercised in this context. It is no accident that judgment is often linked with words like *chesed* and *tsedeq*, which are integral to the whole conception of covenant. 'Maintaining "law" and "justice" is therefore to take care that the true relations are not disturbed (*mishpaṭ*) and that the integrity of each man in the community is maintained fully (*ṣedaqah*). Only thus is the demand of the *chesed* done full justice, and can the Covenant-relation in the people continue to exist.'[3]

God does not leave men to produce *mishpaṭ* from their own resources. He gives them the help they need, so that He may be thought of as the Author of *mishpaṭ* in men. Thus in the specific

---

[1] Cf. H. H. Rowley, 'to Amos justice was of the very essence of God's Being, and therefore it must mark all who worship Him' (*The Growth of the Old Testament*, London, 1950, p. 112).

[2] *Vocabulary of the Bible*, ed. J. J. von Allmen, London, 1958, p. 209.

[3] Th. C. Vriezen, *op. cit.*, p. 327.

case of Solomon, the people saw 'that the wisdom of God was in him, to do judgement' (1 Ki. iii. 28). Jehoshaphat can say to his judges, 'ye judge not for man, but for the Lord; and he is with you in the judgement' (2 Ch. xix. 6). The general principle is that, 'Many seek the ruler's favour: but a man's judgement cometh from the Lord' (Pr. xxix. 26). It is abundantly clear that *mishpaṭ* is not simply the result of human striving. When it appears in men it is the gift of God.[1] The laws are to be seen in this light. *Mishpaṭ* frequently occurs in the sense of a 'law', being usually translated then as 'ordinance'.[2] These 'ordinances' are not the arbitrary enactments of a capricious ruler. Nor are they the concrete expression of some abstract law. They are the merciful provision of a God who loves His people to show them the right way, and to give them the guidance they need as they seek to live in His service. They are the aid provided by a God who loves *mishpaṭ*, and does *mishpaṭ*, so that His people in their turn may also do *mishpaṭ*.

III. THE JUDGMENT OF THE LORD

The Old Testament writers insist that the Lord is active in judging. Over and over they use the various judgment words to describe His activity past, present and future. Few men today would spontaneously use legal phraseology to describe their dealings with God. There is a dislike of 'legalism' and a suspicion of legal categories as means of explaining God's relationship to His people. The Hebrews had no such inhibitions. They exulted in legal imagery and were especially fond of the illustration of a lawsuit wherein God and God's people are on opposite sides

---

[1] Cf. F. W. Dillistone, 'God maintains *mishpaṭ*, and where any relation within the covenant is disturbed, he is concerned to recreate and restore it . . . Men are endued with the Spirit in order that they may establish order and harmonious relations within the covenanted community' (*The Holy Spirit in the Life of Today*, London, 1946, p. 72).

[2] Cf. J. Pedersen, '*mishpaṭ* means 'the law for the actions of mankind . . . And not only the law of mankind; it denotes all law, all lawfulness' (*op. cit.*, I-II, p. 351). So also Delitzsch, *mishpaṭ* 'is fundamental right, right which is raised above the form it assumes at various times and which is always the same' (on Ps. xciv. 15, translated by David Eaton).

(e.g. Is. xli. 1; Je. xii. 1; Mi. vi. 1ff.).[1] They distinguished the Lord's judgment from men's judgment in that the former is perfectly just. Men's judgment was all too fallible. Everyone accepted the idea that the rich and the well connected would not be judged in the same way as the poor and lowly. There was indeed one law for the rich and another for the poor and sometimes this was written into the statutes.[2] But Yahweh's judgment was with perfect justice.[3] 'He shall judge the world in righteousness, he shall minister judgement to the peoples in uprightness' (Ps. ix. 8). This carries a threat to the wicked, for they will certainly be punished. 'I will do unto them after their way, and according to their deserts will I judge them; and they shall know that I am the Lord' (Ezk. vii. 27).

But, though God's judgment will be just, and give the wicked no cause for complaint, we should not think of it as a blind weighing of merits and demerits in a balance. *Mishpaṭ* may take its origin from a legal matrix, but it makes its home with qualities like lovingkindness, faithfulness, righteousness, mercy (or mercies), truth and glory (see Ps. xxxvi. 5f., lxxxix. 14; Ezk. xxxix. 21; Ho. ii. 19, etc.). It is repeatedly linked with qualities like these. It is a blend of reliability and clemency, of law and love. It is a love of men and a love of right. Not the one and not the other,

[1] L. Köhler brings out the God-centred nature of judgment. '*All salvation is to be related to God alone, not to man.* Therefore judgment is also salvation, for judgment is restoration of the honour and holiness (*heiligkeit*) of God. These are injured and diminished by the sin of man. The end judgment has in view is the full restoration of these two things, so that really the whole earth is full of His glory, Isa. 6. 3, and the name of the great king is terrible among the Gentiles, Mal. 1. 14' (*Old Testament Theology*, London, 1957, p. 218).

[2] Thus the Code of Hammurabi provides that 'If a man has put out the eye of a free man, they shall put out his eye. If he breaks the bone of a (free) man, they shall break his bone. If he puts out the eye of a villein or breaks the bone of a villein, he shall pay one maneh of silver' (196-198; *The Babylonian Laws,* ed. G. R. Driver and John C. Miles, ii, Oxford, 1955, p. 77). Something of the same sort appears, of course, among the Hebrews, as when it is laid down that 'thou shalt give life for life, eye for eye, tooth for tooth. . . .' But if it is the eye or the tooth of a slave the master's eye or tooth is not hurt. Instead the slave goes free (Ex. xxi. 23-27).

[3] Shakespeare expresses this point of view,
'Heaven is above all yet; there sits a judge,
That no king can corrupt.'—HENRY VIII, III. i. 99f.

but both.[1] With us legalism has acquired the notion of a soulless, rigid application of the letter of the law to the detriment of human values. Not so did the Hebrews understand judgment. For them law was the bulwark against oppression. The poor and the weak looked to law to save them from the might of the rich and the powerful. 'Save me, O God, by thy name, and judge me in thy might' said the Psalmist (Ps. liv. 1), and such pleas are common. We may put a distinction between kindness and legal processes, but we should be clear that the Hebrews did not.

Yahweh's judgment is to be thought of as the outworking of His mercy and of His wrath. This to us seems something of a contradiction. But in the Old Testament it is the working out of a clear and consistent purpose. God does not change His attitude when He shows mercy at one time and wrath at another, any more than a modern parent when he rewards his child for good behaviour and punishes him for naughtiness. God's purposes are consistently righteous.

This often spells deliverance.[2] The Lord 'doth execute the judgement of the fatherless and widow, and loveth the stranger, in giving him food and raiment' (Dt. x. 18). 'The meek will he guide in judgement: and the meek will he teach his way' (Ps. xxv. 9). Arising out of this are frequent appeals to the Lord to judge, when one is being oppressed, and the formula, 'The Lord judge between me and thee', is a way of protesting one's innocence. By contrast, a state of complete hopelessness is indicated when no judgment may be looked for. Thus Job exclaims despairingly, 'Behold, I cry out of wrong, but I am not heard: I cry for help, but there is no judgement' (Jb. xix. 7).

But the judgment of the Lord means doom for evildoers. Isaiah can think of Jerusalem as being 'purged' by 'the spirit of judgement and by the spirit of burning' (Is. iv. 4). Jeremiah speaks of Yahweh as uttering His judgments (Je. i. 16, iv. 12)—a word from the Lord is sufficient to bring to the wicked the punishment they deserve. And He utters a striking word in Deuteronomy

[1] Cf. Pedersen, 'Right and love belong together' (*op. cit.*, I-II, p. 352).
[2] To E. W. Heaton this is 'of tremendous significance. It meant that, for the prophets, the righteousness of Yahweh embraced both his judgement *on* wickedness and his salvation *from* wickedness' (*op. cit.*, p. 82).

xxxii. 41, 'If I whet my glittering sword, and mine hand take hold on judgement; I will render vengeance to mine adversaries, and will recompense them that hate me.' The plural noun *sh^ephaṭim*, 'judgments', occurs sixteen times, and always of punishments inflicted by the Lord (e.g. Ex. vi. 6; Nu. xxxiii. 4). Especially remarkable is the use of Ezekiel. The word occurs ten times in his prophecy, nine times in speeches of Yahweh as He announces punishments He will inflict. Mostly these refer to Israel (Ezk. v. 10), but also included are Moab (Ezk. xxv. 11), Zidon (Ezk. xxviii. 22), Egypt (Ezk. xxx. 14), and 'those that do despite' to Jacob (Ezk. xxviii. 26). The choice of this word shows that the punishments are not arbitrary. They are the due penalty for evil deeds.

Sometimes men are Yahweh's agents in judgment. Thus in Ezekiel xxiii. 24 He says, 'they shall come against thee with weapons, chariots, and wagons, and with an assembly of peoples; they shall set themselves against thee with buckler and shield and helmet round about: and I will commit the judgement unto them, and they shall judge thee according to their judgements.' This is important for an understanding of much of the Old Testament teaching on judgment. The Babylonians and others had no thought of effecting Yahweh's purpose. They thought of themselves as doing their own will, executing their own judgments. But the prophet saw deeper. He realized that these heathen soldiers were merely Yahweh's instruments. They were the tools He used to bring to pass His judgments on men.

Whether through the agency of men or not, Yahweh's judgment is a process which sifts men. It separates the righteous from the wicked and thus makes the 'remnant' to appear. This points us to a creative element in judgment. We must not think of it as merely negative and destructive. It has, it is true, negative and punitive aspects. But what emerges as the result of judgment is, so to speak, all clear gain. It is the beloved community, and we cannot imagine how this could possibly appear apart from judgment.[1]

---

[1] Cf. J. V. Langmead Casserley, 'To some extent ... the remnant is created by the judgment, for it is in the hour of crisis or judgment that men truly know and make manifest where they ultimately stand. Judgment is creative as well as revelatory' (*Christian Community*, London, 1960, p. 12). So also

[*Continued on next page.*

But the emphasis where Yahweh and judgment are concerned is on the future. In a clear majority of the places where the verb *shaphat* occurs the reference directly or indirectly is to the Lord's judgment. And in most cases the reference is future.[1] While some of these refer to temporal judgments like the exile the conclusion is inescapable that to the men of the Old Testament the most significant thing about judgment was the eschatological judgment of the Lord. For the present the wicked may appear to triumph. Injustice and inequality may abound. Evil men may flourish like the bay tree. But this is only because, in the exercise of His sovereign will, Yahweh allows it. At the end time He will put forth His mighty arm and judge. Sometimes the thought emphasized is that He will judge His people (Ezk. vii. 8), or even a section of His people (Ezk. xxxiv. 20). But more usually there is the thought of a general assize of the nations. 'For he cometh; for he cometh to judge the earth: he shall judge the world with righteousness, and the peoples with his truth' (Ps. xcvi. 13). The frequency of examples of this future use of the concept taken with the comparative fewness of the examples where Yahweh is said actually to have judged men shows that the Hebrews discerned the Lord's judgment not so much in what He has done as in what He will do. It is the expression of faith, rather than of sight.

It is also the expression of a profound conviction that 'the world is out of joint'. The polytheists of the ancient world were, in general, tolerant and contented folk. Somewhere among the multiplicity of the gods they had found a complaisant master, and they were content to drift along with him. Not so the Hebrews. For them every work of man stands under the judgment of God. No state of the world can be accepted which does not conform to His will. That is to say the world must be purged of every evil thing, and the Hebrews expected this only in the end

---

Adam C. Welch, 'The judgment itself may be long; it must be appallingly severe, but it must issue in something larger and richer than mere destruction' (*Kings and Prophets of Israel*, London, 1955, p. 207).

[1] Excluding the participle *shophet* (usually equivalent to a noun, a 'judge'), the verb *shaphat* occurs 135 times, of which 65 apply directly to Yahweh, 2 to the Messiah, and 9 to men as Yahweh's agents. Of the 65 referring to Yahweh, 41 look to the future, as, of course, do the messianic passages.

time, for only then would the judgment of God be seen in its completeness. As G. Ernest Wright puts it, 'A profound disharmony exists between the will of God and the existing social order. God in his redemptive work stands in judgment upon man for his sin, and the startling affirmation is made that man and his society can only be redeemed through the purifying fire of divine judgment.'[1]

This restless dissatisfaction with the world as at present constituted is often overlooked, but it is of fundamental importance for Old Testament thought. The pious Hebrew had always before him the task of 'judgment'. He was to right wrongs, to deliver the oppressed and overthrow the oppressor. But realistically he perceived that no man would ever accomplish this task perfectly. So in faith he looked and longed for the time when God would intervene and perfectly bring to pass the desired end.

[1] *Op. cit.*, p. 45.

CHAPTER II

JUDGMENT IN THE OLD TESTAMENT: WORDS OTHER THAN SHAPHAT

SHAPHAT and its cognates are incomparably the most important and the most frequently used Old Testament words for expressing the idea of judgment. Accordingly we have examined them at some length. But a number of other words reinforce *shaphat*, and we must give attention to those which are rendered by 'judge' or some similar expression.

I. DYN

Brown, Driver and Briggs give the meaning of this verb as 'judge' and they speak of it as a synonym of *shaphat*.[1] When they come to classify the uses of the word they put first 'act as judge, minister judgment'. There is undoubtedly a legal base to this word group, just as is the case with *shaphat* and its relations. But in usage there tends to be some stress on the idea of help or deliverance. *Dyn* almost means 'vindicate'. This is not to deny that there are other and legal uses which may well, as Brown, Driver and Briggs maintain, take us nearer the original meaning. But if we are trying to get the force of the word as used in the Old Testament we cannot overlook this emphasis. We might classify the usage of the word group in this way (taking the noun *dyn* as well as the verb):

1. Deliverance

This is the use found in ten out of twenty-three occurrences of the verb[2] and ten out of twenty of the noun. It may be used of an

[1] Similarly Th. C. Vriezen gives but one meaning for the two verbs: '*din* and *shft* (to bring to justice and to pronounce judgment)' (*op. cit.*, p. 172, n. 2).
[2] I exclude *yadon* in Gn. vi. 3; although both AV and RV render 'strive' as though from *dyn*. G. J. Spurrel cites Joseph Kimchi and Rashi as agreeing with this rendering, but objects to it that 'strive' in the verb *dyn* is the meaning of the Niph'al, not the Qal, and that it depends on the reciprocal force of that conjugation. He also notes that the versions mostly render 'abide'

[*Continued on next page.*]

JUDGMENT—OLD TESTAMENT: WORDS OTHER THAN SHAPHAT 27

actual deliverance wrought by the Lord in time past, as when Rachel exclaimed, after her handmaid bore the child Dan, 'God hath judged me, and hath also heard my voice, and hath given me a son' (Gn. xxx. 6). The child's name, of course, reflects this.[1] Or it may be used in prayer for deliverance, as when the Psalmist prays, 'Save me, O God, by thy name, and judge me in thy might' (Ps. liv. 1). The parallelism with 'save' makes the meaning of *dyn* abundantly clear here. The word is also used of men, sometimes of those who do and sometimes of those who do not 'judge' in this way. Josiah 'judged the cause of the poor and needy' (Je. xxii. 16; both verb and noun are used of him), whereas the 'wicked men' whom Jeremiah castigates, by contrast, 'plead not the cause, the cause of the fatherless, that they should prosper; and the right of the needy do they not judge' (Je. v. 28; again, both noun and verb).

---

or the like, which 'best suits the context, but it does not seem possible to get it out of the present text'. He himself regards the verb as an intransitive form of the imperfect of *dyn* with the meaning 'rule'. The Targums make it synonymous with *dyn* and translate 'judge' (*Notes on the Text of the Book of Genesis*, Oxford, 1896, pp. 70f.). J. Skinner, however, objects to the whole idea that the verb is from *dyn*, pointing out that this root 'shows no trace of med. ן in Heb. . . . and to call it a juss. or intrans. form is an abuse of grammatical language' (*in loc.*). Others take up a similar position. The passage is certainly difficult, but for our present purpose the important point is that there seems no good reason for thinking that the verb is from *dyn*. We may therefore ignore it.

[1] 'The first she named *Dan, i.e.* judge, because God had judged her, *i.e.* procured her justice, hearkened to her voice (prayer), and removed the reproach of childlessness' (C. F. Keil and F. Delitzsch, *in loc.;* Spurrel is similar, as is Delitzsch). S. R. Driver says of the etymologies generally, 'The explanations may in one or two cases be correct: but in most cases they rest merely upon *assonances* . . . it must also remain an open question whether even so the actual origin of the different names is preserved, and whether the explanations offered are not in reality popular etymologies of the names of tribes' (*The Book of Genesis*, London, 1948, p. 272). So C. T. Fritsch, 'for the most part these are purely popular etymologies which are based on resemblances of sound and not on linguistic principles' (*in loc.*). The objection that these are 'popular etymologies' strikes me as somewhat strange. What other kind of etymology can we expect from people like Rachel and Leah? J. Skinner is not as sceptical as some, his comment being, 'the etymology here given (√דין "judge") is very probably correct, the form being an abbreviated theophorous name' (*in loc.*). But whether these etymologies be accepted or not, the writer of Gn. xxx. 6 could use the verb *dyn* of deliverance, and this is the point on which we are concerned to insist.

2. Punishment

This is not a frequent usage (twice of the verb, three times of the noun), but it does occur. Thus Elihu assures Job 'thou art full of the judgement of the wicked: judgement and justice take hold on thee' (Jb. xxxvi. 17), where his meaning is that the sufferings of the patriarch are God's judgment on him for his wickedness.[1]

3. Calling to account

There are places where the Lord is said to judge His people, but it is not clear whether in punishing or delivering. If the point can be determined, then this grouping will disappear and be absorbed in the previous two. If it cannot, then it is a reminder that judgment, though it may issue in reward and deliverance or in punishment and condemnation, is yet the working out of one consistent divine purpose. If we may cite Elihu once more, he goes on to inform Job that 'by these (i.e. rain, etc.) he judgeth the peoples; he giveth meat in abundance. He covereth his hands with the lightning; and giveth it a charge that it strike the mark' (Jb. xxxvi. 31f.). Judgment here is God's activity in sending the weather. He does not do this at haphazard, but sends such weather as to give abundant supplies of food to the righteous, while He launches His thunderbolts against the wicked.[2]

4. Engage in a lawsuit, Strive

'The Lord standeth up to plead, and standeth to judge the peoples' (Is. iii. 13; *dyn*='judge') is the language of the law-court.[3] This is in accordance with a persistent tendency in the Old Testament to illustrate relations between God and His

---

[1] 'Job had joined the sinners in their judgment of God, and therefore God's judgment must keep its hold upon him' (E. C. S. Gibson, *in loc.*).

[2] Cf. A. B. Davidson, 'He judges the peoples by the lightning and the rain cloud. By the one He "scatters" and "discomfits" His enemies (Ps. xviii. 14), and by the other He watereth the earth and makes it fruitful (Is. lv. 10)' (*in loc.*).

[3] 'A judgment scene . . . expressing in another form the same sympathy with the oppressed which appears in *v.* 12. Jehóvah, at once accuser and judge, comes to vindicate the cause of the poor against their oppressors' (J. Skinner, *in loc.*).

people with legal imagery. But lawsuits often mean bitter conflict, and the word *dyn* is thus used on occasion to denote strife even where there is no legal point at issue. Thus we read in 2 Samuel xix. 9 that, after the slaying of Absalom, 'all the people were at strife throughout all the tribes of Israel', and again we are advised, 'Cast out the scorner, and contention shall go out; yea, strife and ignominy shall cease' (Pr. xxii. 10).

5. Rule

In accordance with one aspect of *shaphaṭ* this word group also can mean 'rule' on occasion. Thus the prophet speaks the word of the Lord to Joshua, 'If thou wilt walk in my ways, and if thou wilt keep my charge, then thou also shalt judge my house . . .' (Zc. iii. 7).[1] For the noun, used without possibility of mistaking the meaning, let us notice the expression, 'A king that sitteth on the throne of judgement' (Pr. xx. 8). Though this use is found, there is no real evidence for thinking that here, any more than in the case of *shaphaṭ*, does 'rule' give the basic meaning.

We might sum up the usage of the word group by saying that it reinforces and underlines some of what we have seen to be the meaning conveyed by *shaphaṭ*. It perhaps lends a new emphasis to the salvation aspect of judgment. It certainly reminds us again that the Old Testament concept of judgment has a stubborn legal basis, arising as it does from that judicial activity of discrimination in accordance with right which separates the righteous from the wicked and takes action as a result.

II. PLL

This interesting verb is used in the Pi'el in the sense 'to judge', and in the Hithpa'el with the meaning 'to pray'. Both conjugations are used in 1 Samuel ii. 25, and it may help us to get the sense of it if we look briefly at this passage. Eli says to his sons, 'If one man sin against another, God shall judge him

---

[1] David Kimchi explains this, 'Inasmuch as he was High-Priest, and the other priests were to act by his command' (*in loc.*). H. G. Mitchell translates, 'thou shalt rule my house' and comments: 'The house, of course, is the temple . . . The declaration here made, therefore, amounts to a charter granting to Joshua and his successors a sole and complete control in matters of religion' (*I.C.C., in loc.*).

(*wuphil'lo*): but if a man sin against the Lord, who shall intreat (*yithpallel*) for him?' It is likely that we should understand '*elohim* in this verse as 'the judge' (RV mg.) or 'the judges'. If the word is taken as referring to the Deity at least He will be acting through the judges. Eli is saying then that there is the possibility of redress through the recognized channels if a man sins against his fellow, but for the kind of sin that his sons were committing, a sin against God Himself, there is no possibility of anyone becoming mediator. In a case of this sort no intercession can avail.

The basic meaning of the root is probably something like 'intervene, interpose'.[1] This intervention may take place when there is a dispute between men. In that case it will be for the purpose of settling the matter. While theoretically this might lead to the word's being used either for vindication or for condemnation (both will follow: one of the parties will be vindicated and the other condemned), in practice the word is always used of punishment. Some other verb is used to express the thought of vindication. If the dispute is between God and men then no human is in a position to act as mediator. Man will always be in the wrong, for God is by definition perfectly just, perfectly righteous. There is but one course open to any would-be mediator, namely to pray. S. R. Driver understands the passage from 1 Samuel in much this way. He takes the Pi'el to signify 'to mediate' and he cites as an example the mediation we see in Psalm cvi. 30 ('Then stood up Phinehas, and executed judgement'). Since Phinehas 'executed judgement' by slaying Zimri and Cozbi the kind of 'mediation' contemplated by *wayᵉphallel* is punishment for wrongdoing. Driver thinks of the Hithpa'el as meaning '*to interpose as mediator*, specially by means of entreaty', and he cites Genesis xx. 17 ('And Abraham prayed unto God: and God healed Abimelech, and his wife . . .').[2]

---

[1] Brown, Driver and Briggs, *sub voce*. They add, 'hence both *arbitrate, judge* and *intercede, pray*'.

[2] *Notes on the Hebrew Text of the Books of Samuel*, Oxford, 1913, p. 35. C. F. Keil and F. Delitzsch think of the Pi'el as signifying 'to decide or pass sentence', and they cite Gn. xlviii. 11 ('I had not thought to see thy face: and, lo, God hath let me see thy seed also'). Then the verb comes to mean, 'to arbitrate, to settle a dispute as arbitrator (Ezek. xvi. 52, Ps. cvi. 30)'. In the

[*Continued on next page.*]

From the use of this verb, then, it would seem that we can notice two points of importance for our present purpose. The first is that the basic meaning has to do with intervention. That is to say, the initiative comes from outside. Left to themselves, men would never undergo judgment, not at any rate the final judgment. But they are not left to themselves. There will be intervention and that from God Himself. The second point is that the verb is always used of the kind of intervention that results in the punishment of the wrongdoer. It is often claimed that the meaning of the word has to do with arbitration and the like, but the usage is always for the punishment of the wicked. We are reminded that sin is serious.[1]

III. YKH̠

Brown, Driver and Briggs give the meaning of this verb as '*decide, adjudge, prove* (NH Pi. *argue with*)', while Köhler lists eight meanings, beginning with '1. reprove . . . 2. argue before . . .' The word denotes a rather more argumentative process than those with which we have so far had to do. There is often the idea of discussion or argument, though with a somewhat condemnatory air, for one shows another to be in the wrong. It is possible to get lost in the multiplicity of meanings, so we will select three points as important for our present inquiry.

1. The word means 'judge'

There are undoubtedly passages in which the word has the meaning 'judge' even though these may not be basic for the meaning of the word group. But they show that it does give us part of

---

Hithpaʻel they see the meaning as 'to act as mediator, hence to entreat', and they give the meaning of the passage as 'In the case of one man's sin against another, God settles the dispute as arbitrator through the proper authorities; whereas, when a man sins against God, no one can interpose as arbitrator. Such a sin cannot be disposed of by intercession' (*in loc.*). It seems to me that Gn. xlviii. 11 is a difficult verse from which to derive the thought of arbitration. Moreover, in 1 Sa. ii. 25 the thought is surely that of punishing the wrongdoer rather than simply that of arbitrating. Thus an interpretation of the kind favoured by Driver is more likely to be correct.

[1] Nouns from this root, like *tᵉphillah* or *palil*, are always used of prayer or of judgment, not of both. And where judgment is the meaning it is judgment in the sense of condemnation, not of deliverance.

the Old Testament view of judgment, and its peculiar quantum of meaning is thus not to be overlooked. For an example, let us look at the incident wherein, after Laban has searched through Jacob's belongings for his missing teraphim, that patriarch is moved to reply: 'Whereas thou hast felt about all my stuff, what hast thou found of all thy household stuff? Set it here before my brethren and thy brethren, that they may judge betwixt us two' (Gn. xxxi. 37). We discern here the authentic meaning of 'judge'. Jacob is inviting Laban to submit to a process wherein his 'brethren' and Jacob's 'brethren' discriminate between the two of them.[1]

2. The word predominantly means 'reprove'

But if there are undoubtedly passages in which the meaning 'judge' cannot be gainsaid, it is also true that the predominant meaning is not there. A concordance shows that the word is more often used of rebuking and the like than of anything else. The tendency is to stress the ill desert of the evil-doer. Thus Abraham 'reproved Abimelech because of the well of water, which Abimelech's servants had violently taken away' (Gn. xxi. 25). The Psalmist characterizes Yahweh as 'He that chastiseth the nations' (Ps. xciv. 10),[2] and again we read that as Jacob's descendants 'went about from nation to nation . . . he suffered no man to do them wrong; yea, he reproved kings for their sakes' (Ps. cv. 13f.). Again, Job told his tormentors, 'He will surely reprove you, if ye do secretly respect persons' (Jb. xiii. 10). There cannot be the slightest doubt but that this word is employed predominantly where condemnation of one sort or another is in mind.

3. Judgment is reasonable

The great point which we learn from *ykh* and which is not brought out so clearly in the other words (though, of course, it is always

---

[1] Cf. H. C. Leupold, 'The kinsmen can serve as arbiters or judges to render a public verdict, which must be all the more fair because it will be a jury composed of adherents of both parties' (*in loc.*).

[2] F. Delitzsch speaks of God's rule as being 'as far as possible from being in connivance with evil' and God consequently is 'one who is able to punish and who does not suffer that which is displeasing to Him to go unpunished' (*in loc.*).

implied), is that judgment is a reasonable process. There are many passages where this verb plainly denotes 'to reason' or the like. It is used, for example, in the well-known passage in the opening chapter of Isaiah, 'Come now, and let us reason together, saith the Lord . . .' (Is. i. 18), after which the prophet goes on to outline the way in which men would find their sins wiped away, and that in which they could look for nothing other than destruction.[1] It is used of Job's desire to put his case before God, 'I desire to reason with God' (Jb. xiii. 3), and of God's case against Israel, 'the Lord hath a controversy with his people, and he will plead (*yithwakkaḥ*) with Israel' (Mi. vi. 2). In view of the attitude of some people today towards the conception of divine judgment it is worth stressing that on the Old Testament view the whole process is eminently reasonable. We should not think of a capricious God arbitrarily handing out penalties and rewards, or even of the process of judgment as something which might have been otherwise had God chosen to let matters slide. Jeremiah reminded the men of his day that 'Thine own wickedness shall correct thee, and thy backslidings shall reprove (*tokhiḥukh*) thee' (Je. ii. 19). The nature of life and of the moral struggle and of the eternal law of righteousness mean that judgment is the most reasonable thing imaginable.[2] It is impossible to envisage a process which does away with it and which does not result in chaos.

IV. 'ELOHIM

It is disputed whether this term, which is the usual word for 'God' or for 'gods', should not be understood in some places of the judges. It is translated 'the judges' in the Authorized Version in Exodus xxi. 6, xxii. 8, 9, 9, and in the margin of Exodus xxii. 28, while the singular is employed in 1 Samuel ii. 25.

---

[1] G. B. Gray cites Rashi's comment on the verb, '*i.e.* I and you together, that we may know who has wronged whom' (I.C.C. *in loc.*; Rashi's interpretation goes on, 'and if it is you who have wronged me, I will yet give you hope of repentance'). J. Skinner thinks that 'The idea is that of a legal process in which each party maintains his own case' (*in loc.*).

[2] 'The prophets always attempt to make it clear in their testimony that the punishments inflicted by God completely fit the sins of the people . . . they also try to convince the people of the foolishness of sin' (Th. C. Vriezen, *op. cit.*, p. 274).

In all these passages except the last the Revised Version reads 'God' in the text and 'the judges' in the margin, while in the last the marginal reading is in the singular, 'the judge'. There does not seem much doubt but that the judicial processes are envisaged in all these passages, however we translate the term.[1] Nor need we doubt that the judicial process is seen as something of a high dignity and to be performed only as in the sight of God. Brown, Driver and Briggs give as the first meaning of the word, '*rulers, judges,* either as divine representatives at sacred places or as reflecting divine majesty and power'. Either way judgment is closely linked with God. It is a divine prerogative. We ought not to be in any doubt but that judgment is a majestic process, nor that all human judgment points us back (and on) to the judgment of God.

Traditionally the references to 'the gods' in Psalm lxxxii have been taken in the same way. Thus F. Delitzsch understands it of 'magistrates' who 'are the feudatories and bearers of the image of God, and as being His representatives are therefore also themselves called אלהים'.[2] In more recent times the trend among Old Testament scholars is to understand the Psalm as showing a

[1] '*Elohim* in such passages is difficult, and it is not surprising accordingly that the most diverse views have been held. Thus S. R. Driver, on 1 Sa. ii. 25, says the term signifies 'not the judge as such, but the judge *as the mouthpiece of a Divine sentence*', which seems to refer the word to the judge, though closely associating him with the divine. On Ex. xxi. 6 he says that the translation 'the judges' 'is only a paraphrase; for though God, in cases such as the present, may be conceived as acting through a judge, as His representative or mouthpiece, that does not make "Elohim" *mean* "judge", or "judges".' More recently E. Jacob has written, 'we do not think that (Elohim) was ever applied to human beings' (*op. cit.*, p. 98, n. 2; he makes one exception, viz. Ps. xlv). A. H. McNeile thinks the term 'a vague one, which it is better to understand as including the sanctuary and all connected with it' (on Ex. xxi. 6). J. P. Lange rejects the idea that it refers to priests and thinks of 'the court of the assembly, which passed judgment in the name of God' (on Ex. xxi. 6). A. F. Kirkpatrick says, 'Judges, as the representatives of God in executing justice on earth (Deut. i. 17), are sometimes styled *gods* . . . but it seems best not to limit the present passage to human judgments' (on 1 Sa. ii. 25). The LXX renders in Ex. xxi. 6 with πρὸς τὸ κριτήριον τοῦ Θεοῦ.

[2] *In loc.* He notices that the Targums support this with their rendering *dayyanayya'*. More recently E. J. Kissane introduces his discussion of Ps. lxxxii with 'the main part of the poem is a denunciation of the corrupt judges', and he comments on verse 6, 'The psalmist has called the judges

[*Continued on next page.*]

belief in the real existence of the gods of the heathen. They are subordinate to Yahweh, and He can call them to account, but they are real beings. Thus Aubrey R. Johnson says that the Psalm 'introduces us at the outset to the heavenly court, and reveals Yahweh as pronouncing sentence upon the assembled gods of the nations because of their misrule'. Because of this, 'despite their standing as the sons of God, Yahweh goes on to pronounce what must be the final sentence upon them for failing to live up to this ideal, decreeing that as a result they shall die like ordinary human beings'.[1] I am not convinced by this reasoning, and that for a number of reasons. It would be against the consistent monotheism of the Old Testament, and it should not be forgotten that the Psalm was recognized as canonical by a long succession of convinced monotheists. Again, there are the passages we have considered earlier in this section, which seem to me to indicate that the term *'elohim* on occasion was used of the judges. Then there is the language of the passage itself. Consider verses 2ff:

'How long will ye judge unjustly,
And respect the persons of the wicked?
Judge the poor and fatherless:
Do justice to the afflicted and destitute.
Rescue the poor and needy:
Deliver them out of the hand of the wicked.'

"gods", and by virtue of their office they deserve that title; for they are God's representatives'. C. A. and E. G. Briggs refer the Psalm to 'the wicked governors of the nations holding Israel in subjection . . . All of these are called gods, because as rulers and judges they reflect the divine majesty of Law and order in government' (*I.C.C., in loc.*).

[1] *Sacral Kingship in Ancient Israel*, Cardiff, 1955, pp. 89, 90. So also G. Widengren, 'Yahweh is accordingly the highest god in a council or assembly of gods, called "the Holy Ones", or "the Holy Ones of God" or simply "the gods"' (*Myth, Ritual and Kingship*, ed. S. H. Hooke, Oxford, 1958, p. 161). E. Jacob says, 'Yahweh is represented as exercising judgment in the assembly of the gods and reducing the latter to the rank of angels or princes for not having exercised justice' (*op. cit.*, p. 66). Th. C. Vriezen thinks there is a polytheistic background, but he understands the Psalm of 'divine beings' subordinate to Yahweh. 'The conception of God includes . . . the idea of a heavenly host, of a mighty army of divine beings surrounding Him . . . Yahweh is a unique God, but He is not alone' (*op. cit.*, p. 180).

This is consistent with the activity required of the judges throughout the Old Testament. But such functions are not sought from nor expected of the heathen gods. This point does not seem to me to be given adequate consideration by those scholars who understand the passage of the gods. There are not wanting in the Old Testament passages referring to the gods of the heathen. But where are they spoken of in terms like this? The Psalm looks to me much better understood of human judges. In verse 1 God calls them to account. In verses 6f. He reminds them of their mortality:

'I said, Ye are gods,
And all of you sons of the Most High.
Nevertheless ye shall die like men,
And fall like one of the princes.'

These statements are not relevant to the gods of the nations. Nor is the final verse which calls on God to judge 'the earth', i.e. the abode of the judges, not that of the gods.[1]

But, whatever be the verdict in Psalm lxxxii, both this and the passages previously noted clearly link the function of judging with the divine. They thus invest it with dignity and serious purpose.[2]

V. PQD

This is a verb with multitudinous meanings, a subordinate one being 'judge'. Brown, Driver and Briggs list it as 'attend to, visit, muster, appoint', a definition which shows that the word ranges over a good deal of territory. Köhler gives the original meaning as 'miss, worry about', then 'look after, go to see'. This is supported to some extent by the usage in the cognate languages, which seems often to be that of 'caring' or of 'missing'. What is clear is that the word has many meanings, one of which (and quite a common one) is 'to visit'. And this meaning gives rise to one or two others, for visiting may be done with more results than one.

[1] For many the decisive criterion will be the fact that our Lord understood the term to refer to them 'unto whom the word of God came' (Jn. x. 35).
[2] It is possible that *elohim* should be understood of the judges also in Ps. cxxxviii. 1, as F. Delitzsch and W. E. Barnes hold. The latter cites the Targum in support of this view, and explains the passage thus: 'The Psalmist means that he will not be ashamed to acknowledge Jehovah's benefits before the highest authorities of his people' (*in loc.*).

JUDGMENT—OLD TESTAMENT: WORDS OTHER THAN SHAPHAT 37

Thus the word is used in a good sense, as when, on the occasion of the birth of Isaac, we read: 'And the Lord visited[1] Sarah as he had said, and the Lord did unto Sarah as he had spoken' (Gn. xxi. 1). Not a few passages might be cited in which this verb is used of visiting with blessing in this way. But if God visits a man or a nation, and that man or nation is sinful, then the result of the visit will be different. Thus Jeremiah, after giving an account of the sins of his nation, proceeds: 'Shall I not visit for these things? saith the Lord: and shall not my soul be avenged on such a nation as this?' (Je. v. 9; the expression is repeated in verse 29). The same prophet says: 'Even so have they loved to wander; they have not refrained their feet: therefore the Lord doth not accept them; now will he remember their iniquity, and visit their sins' (Je. xiv. 10). The verb is sometimes translated in terms of judgment as in Jeremiah li. 47, 'Therefore, behold, the days come, that I will do judgement upon the graven images of Babylon . . .'

From all this we must be reminded of one important truth. God is not, and cannot be neutral.[2] For God to visit is the same thing as for Him to look graciously on the righteous and the needy, and to punish the wicked.

VI. RIBH

Unlike the words we have looked at so far, *ribh* is not translated by 'judge' or the like. But it is clearly relevant to our study, for it refers to lawsuits in many, perhaps most, of its occurrences.[3] Its basic meaning has to do with strife, which lends itself to the thought of parties contending in a lawsuit. Thus it is used both in contexts where judgment is in question, and in some where there is no thought of any legal process. We examine its uses in order.

---

[1] '*Visited*—viz. with favour and blessing' (S. R. Driver, *in loc.*). H. C. Leupold comments, 'God's drawing near to one, whether in mercy or in severity, is described by the term; and it always involves that some token of His attitude is distinctly in evidence after His visitation' (*in loc.*).

[2] 'God's holiness is a consuming fire and cannot bear the existence of sin' (Th. C. Vriezen, *op. cit.*, p. 275).

[3] The uncertainty arises because there are passages where the word occurs in which it is not absolutely clear whether the conflict is a legal one, e.g. Is. xlv. 9, 'Woe unto him that striveth with his Maker!'

1. Strive, dispute

This appears to be the fundamental meaning of the word group. Brown, Driver and Briggs give 'strive, contend' as the main meaning, and they go on to cite words from the cognate languages with meanings like 'agitate', 'disquiet', 'cry', 'shout', 'quarrel noisily', etc. Sometimes the thought of bodily violence is present, as in Moses' blessing of Judah: 'with his hands he contended for himself' (Dt. xxxiii. 7).[1] More usually, as Köhler notes, the meaning is a strife in words,[2] as when certain waters were named 'Meribah; because the children of Israel strove with the Lord' (Nu. xx. 13; in verse 3 the words with which they 'strove' are given).[3]

2. Complain, rebuke

Arising from the thought of strife is that of complaint or of rebuke. Here there is not so much the idea of a quarrel with reciprocal action, as of one person taking the initiative and speaking his mind about the other. The passage wherein Jacob 'was wroth, and chode with Laban' (Gn. xxxi. 36) is a good illustration, as is that wherein Nehemiah 'contended with' (AV 'rebuked') the nobles (Ne. v. 7).

3. Conduct a lawsuit

But the most important use of the word group is found when it describes a lawsuit of some kind (often a figurative one, with Yahweh pictured as taking legal action against His people). This kind of usage will account for nearly half of the total

---

[1] Keil and Delitzsch take the meaning to be 'With his hands... is he fighting for it (the nation)'. Even so, the main point is that the strife in question is with the hands.

[2] He gives as the first meaning of the word '(with words, complaints, assertions, contestings, reproaches) contend; conduct a (legal) case, suit'.

[3] The expression 'king Jareb' (Ho. v. 13, x. 6) is difficult. Probably G. A. Smith is right in giving the meaning as 'King Combative, King Pick-Quarrel' (*in loc.*), in which case the title gives us a good example of the meaning of the word group. A. R. Fausset prefers the meaning, 'The Assyrian "king", ever ready, for his own aggrandizement, to mix himself up with the affairs of neighbouring states, professed to *undertake* Israel's and Judah's *cause*' (*in loc.*).

occurrences of both verb and noun (30 out of 68 occurrences of the verb, and 26 out of 62 of the noun). We see the ordinary processes of law when it is commanded: 'neither shalt thou speak in a cause to turn aside after a multitude to wrest judgement: neither shalt thou favour a poor man in his cause' (Ex. xxiii. 2f.), or when Absalom intervened when 'any man had a suit which should come to the king for judgement' (2 Sa. xv. 2).

But the really significant passages are those wherein Yahweh features in the lawsuit. Sometimes it is said that God has acted. When David heard of Nabal's death, he exclaimed, 'Blessed be the Lord, that hath pleaded the cause of my reproach . . .' (1 Sa. xxv. 39).[1] Here the Lord has already done what was required. David simply rejoices in the fact. But sometimes also it is by way of prayer for future help, as when the Psalmist said, 'Judge me, O God, and plead my cause against an ungodly nation: O deliver me from the deceitful and unjust man' (Ps. xliii. 1). He confidently appeals to the Lord. He looks for vindication and deliverance, but the language in which his appeal is couched is that of the lawcourt. It is not altogether surprising that God's people are exhorted to produce the same kind of conduct themselves: 'judge the fatherless, plead for the widow' (Is. i. 17).

Perhaps nowhere do we get the peculiar flavour of this word better than in the court scene so powerfully depicted by Micah. 'Hear ye now what the Lord saith: Arise, contend thou before the mountains, and let the hills hear thy voice. Hear, O ye mountains the Lord's controversy, and ye enduring foundations of the earth: for the Lord hath a controversy with his people, and he will plead with Israel' (Mi. vi. 1f.; 'contend' and 'controversy' are from this root). Then the prophet goes on to give the words in which the Lord formulates His legal plaint against His people.[2]

[1] Cf. H. P. Smith, 'a quarrel between men of the same blood should be referred to an arbitrator. One element of David's rejoicing is that Yahweh has so promptly assumed this office' (*I.C.C.*, *in loc.*).

[2] G. A. Smith maintains that 'The main idea of the passage . . . is the Trial itself' and he goes on to point out that the imagery of a trial 'sprang by revolt against mechanical and sensational ideas of religion. It emphasised religion as rational and moral . . . God spoke with the people whom He had educated: He pled with them, listened to their statements and questions, and produced His own evidences and reasons. Religion, such a passage as this asserts—religion is not a thing of authority nor of ceremonial nor of

[*Continued on next page.*]

In this way Micah brings out with emphasis the reality of the nation's sin (it is proved up to the hilt: the proof will stand up in a court of law), and the seriousness of that sin (sentence will inevitably be passed on those adjudged guilty). Isaiah makes similar use of this imagery, 'The Lord standeth up to plead, and standeth to judge the peoples' (Is. iii. 13).[1] So does Jeremiah, 'I will yet plead with you, saith the Lord, and with your children's children will I plead' (Je. ii. 9). This prophet also uses our verb to show the hopelessness of the people's case. 'Wherefore will ye plead with me? ye all have transgressed against me, saith the Lord' (Je. ii. 29). The imagery is frequent in Job, e.g., 'I will say unto God, Do not condemn me; shew me wherefore thou contendest with me' (Jb. x. 2), and elsewhere.

Ribh, then, stresses two aspects of judgment. One is the reality of the opposition. A word which originally means 'strife' does not picture God as mildly displeased with sinners. He is radically opposed to all that is evil. Sinners must not be complacent about their position. The other is that God does not act in arbitrary fashion as He deals with sin. Those who feel His hand upon them in judgment may know that their evil deeds are completely proven. The case against them is crystal clear.

There is one further thought, and, though it does not receive much emphasis, it is important. We find it in the last chapter of Micah, where the prophet says, 'I will bear the indignation of the Lord, because I have sinned against him; until he plead my cause . . .' (Mi. vii. 9). Sin must be punished. Justice demands

---

mere feeling, but of argument, reasonable presentation and debate' (*in loc.*). Cf. John Bright, 'In a classic passage (ch. 6: 1-8) he (i.e. Micah) imagined Yahweh entering his case against his people, who had forgotten his gracious acts toward them in the past, and also that his demands—which are just and merciful behaviour and humble obedience—cannot possibly be satisfied by any conceivable heightening of cultic activity. Micah pronounced a doom on Judah of total proportions' (*A History of Israel*, London, 1960, p. 277).

[1] Cf. F. Delitzsch, 'His pleading ריב (Jer. xxv. 31) is, however, at the same time a judging דין; because His accusation, which is absolutely incontestable, is also already the sentence of judgment. Thus He stands in the midst of the peoples (Ps. vii. 8), accuser, judge, and executioner in one person' (*in loc.*).

that.¹ But the final hope of the prophet is with the Lord. He bears God's chastening judgments, and in faith he looks to God to plead his cause.

VII. OTHER WORDS

We have not succeeded in eliciting the whole of the Old Testament teaching on judgment when we have patiently worked through all the judgment words in a concordance. We can learn a good deal about judgment by this process, and, indeed, without the patient sifting of all the evidence it is not possible to speak with any authority on the subject. *Ex cathedra* pronouncements based on isolated texts or passages are of little worth. But when we have looked at all the 'judgment' passages we have not exhausted the theme. The idea is sometimes present when none of the judgment words occurs. Thus, when we read, 'the light of Israel shall be for a fire, and his Holy One for a flame: and it shall burn and devour his thorns and his briers in one day' (Is. x. 17), we are reminded that Israel's relationship to God, regarded as a holy God, necessarily implies judgment.² Or again, Amos can warn the people, 'Therefore thus will I do unto thee, O Israel: and because I will do this unto thee, prepare to meet thy God, O Israel' (Am. iv. 12). Here we find none of the judgment words, but how are we to interpret the passage apart from the thought of an impending judgment?³

---

¹ E. B. Pusey draws attention to the difference between the justice of God and the injustice of those who oppress His people: 'The judgments which God righteously sends, and which man suffers righteously from Him, are unrighteously inflicted by those whose malice He overrules', and thus 'The close of the chastisements of His people is the beginning of the punishment of *their* misdeeds, who used amiss the power which God gave them over it' (*in loc.*).

² Cf. E. Jacob, 'This association, which rests upon election, implies that the holiness of which Israel is the object can turn against them and in certain circumstances in the course of history the divine holiness was for Israel an effective manifestation of judgment' (*op. cit.*, p. 90).

³ There is dispute as to whether these words are basically an appeal or a threat. W. R. Harper takes the former line: 'It is, in accordance with the whole spirit and purpose of prophecy, a call to repentance' (*I.C.C., in loc.*). E. A. Edghill has it both ways. On the one hand, 'Amos has told of God's discipline of His people. All has failed. Nothing remains but utter destruction. ... *Thus* cannot refer to anything but to the overwhelming judgement which

[Continued on next page.

But perhaps the most important concept in this connection is that of 'the day of the Lord'. When we first meet this term the prophet Amos does not stay to explain it, but introduces it as well known. It was evidently a very early idea.[1] 'Woe unto you that desire the day of the Lord! wherefore would ye have the day of the Lord? it is darkness, and not light. As if a man did flee from a lion, and a bear met him; or went into the house and leaned his hand on the wall, and a serpent bit him' (Am. v. 18f.). It seems clear that in popular expectation 'the day of the Lord' was the day when Israel's God would act obviously and unmistakably and show that He was on Israel's side.[2] He would deliver them from every oppressor, and, indeed, deliver every oppressor into their hand.[3] But Amos has a different message. God says to the nation, 'You only have I known of all the families of the earth: therefore I will visit upon you all your iniquities' (Am. iii. 2). Precisely because they stand in a special relationship

is yet to be pronounced', and on the other, '*prepare to meet thy God* cannot mean prepare for the worst . . . The purpose of all prophecy, however unconditional, is to drive men back to God . . . There is always hope in repentance' (*in loc.*). R. S. Cripps in his commentary points out that in the view of many it is 'a solemn warning, the spiritual application of the prediction of judgment upon the nation Israel'. But in an Additional Note (pp. 296f.) he favours the meaning 'be prepared for (*i.e.* await) the worst'. Whichever view we adopt the words are meaningless apart from the thought of impending judgment.

[1] H. H. Rowley says, 'It is increasingly recognized that this element was found in (Israel's) thought from an early age', and he quotes J. M. P. Smith, 'The development of the idea of the Day of Yahweh in Israelitish history was marked, not so much by the addition from time to time of new features as by the expansion and deepening of elements already present, at least in germ, at the time of the origin of the prophetic conception' (*The Faith of Israel*, London, 1956, p. 177 and n.). S. Mowinckel sees the original meaning of the term as 'the day of His manifestation or epiphany, the day of His festival' (*op. cit.*, p. 145). Similarly Pidoux thinks of a festal occasion with the king playing the rôle of divine Judge (*op. cit.*). If this can be accepted it will explain the popular use.

[2] Cf. J. E. Fison, 'for the people as a whole the day of the Lord, or the day of Yahweh, was not really Yahweh's day at all, but Israel's. It was the national trump card which would then be played even though Yahweh might be the player' (*The Christian Hope*, London, 1954, p. 90).

[3] G. Ernest Wright says, 'The optimism of the prosperous in every age produces the illusion that there will be a utopia without judgment' (*The Challenge of Israel's Faith*, London, 1946, p. 102). He also draws attention to

[*Continued on next page.*]

to God they must expect to be judged by a high standard, and punished when they fall short. All men stand under the judgment of God. But especially do God's people stand under His judgment. Notice that this, and not the idea of judgment, was Amos' contribution to the subject. As H. H. Rowley has said, 'This element of judgement belongs essentially to the thought of the Day of the Lord. What Amos brought to the term was not the idea of judgement, but the idea of a moral judgement. It was not to be simply a judgement on Israel's foes, but a judgement on men whose lives were offensive to God, whether within Israel or without.'[1] This truth is reiterated throughout the 'day of the Lord' passages. God has no favourites. His judgment will inevitably fall on all mankind. It is no accident that the last word in our printed Old Testament is a word of judgment.

---

judgment as both present and future, saying that the Day of the Lord 'is always present for those who have eyes to see it, and *yet it is ever about to come*. The judgment of God is always upon us, though we become aware of it when we find ourselves in a crisis' (*op. cit.*, p. 107).

[1] *Op. cit.*, p. 178.

CHAPTER III

JUDGMENT IN THE NEW TESTAMENT: A PRESENT REALITY

I. INTRODUCTION

THE basic judgment word in the New Testament is the verb *krinō*, 'to judge'. Properly this word, as with its English equivalent, applies to a legal process. We see this in Matthew v. 40, 'if any man would go to law with thee...' (cf. also 1 Cor. vi. 1, 6). From this it comes to be used in a non-technical sense of making a decision (again, just as with us). We see this in the reply of Peter and John to the council, 'Whether it be right in the sight of God to hearken unto you rather than unto God, judge ye' (Acts iv. 19). Occasionally there are overtones of Old Testament usages, as in the use now and then for ruling (Mt. xix. 28; Lk. xxii. 30).

More striking, and more important, is the use of the term in connection with Christ's victory over all the forces of evil. This is quite in the manner of the Old Testament passages referring to deliverance. Thus Jesus said, with the cross looming before Him, 'Now is the judgement of this world: now shall the prince of this world be cast out' (Jn. xii. 31). Again He said that the Holy Spirit would 'convict the world in respect of... judgement', and He went on to explain this, 'of judgement, because the prince of this world hath been judged' (Jn. xvi. 8-11). The death of Christ was in one aspect a judicial dealing with the evil one.[1] As in the Old Testament, this does not mean an impartial weighing of evidence. It is a vigorous dealing with evil. The Lord is active in saving His people. But, also as in the Old Testament, there is the thought that God's dealing with Satan is not arbitrary. His overthrow is in accord with justice. He is cast out because he deserves to be cast out. Believers may know that their deliverance is soundly based.

[1] 'In the Cross not Jesus but the devil was *judged*' (A. M. Hunter, *Introducing New Testament Theology*, London, 1957, p. 140).

II. THE PRESENT JUDGMENT OF THE FATHER

The New Testament makes it clear that God is engaged upon a present activity of judging. Sometimes we have a general proposition like 'there is one that seeketh and judgeth' (Jn. viii. 50). This might well be held to apply to the final judgment, and it certainly has its relevance thereto. But it seems better to understand it of a process which is going on in the here and now. It is true that God is the one Judge, and that in the last day that will be made manifest. But it is also true that here and now men may know that their actions are weighed by one Judge, and action taken accordingly.[1] It is this which gives moral significance to history. Unless God is active in present judgment we are shut up to the idea that for this life the moral outcome of our actions has no importance.

Paul makes an important point with regard to this present judgment. He is dealing with the Holy Communion, and points out that because of a wrong use of the sacrament 'many among you are weak and sickly, and not a few sleep' (1 Cor. xi. 30). Then he goes on, 'But if we discerned (*diekrinomen*) ourselves, we should not be judged'. His verb means 'to distinguish', 'to discriminate'. Paul is saying that if we distinguished between what we are and what we ought to be we should avoid the kind of judgment of which he has been speaking.[2] In other words he sees these judgments, not as something simply to be feared and hated, but as incentives to self-examination and right living. An understanding of the activity of the Lord in judging His people here and now can be a powerful incentive to Christian men. It gives a dignity and a meaning to all of life. Everywhere in

---

[1] B. F. Westcott reminds us that this judgment is not recognized by unbelievers. 'None but believers saw the Risen Christ during the forty days: none but believers see Christ in the great changes of human affairs.' But he adds, 'But beyond all these preparatory comings there is a day when "every eye shall see Him, and they also which pierced Him"' (*The Historic Faith*, London and Cambridge, 1883, p. 95).

[2] This activity marks the mature Christian. Shakespeare makes Cleopatra refer to   'My salad days,
    When I was green in judgment.'—ANTONY AND
                                    CLEOPATRA, I. v. 73f.).
The mature Christian will avoid the rash judgments of 'salad days'. His judgment is the outcome of his dependence on God.

the Bible judgment has this characteristic. It incites men to self-examination and repentance. It is never merely a threat.

Paul draws a second conclusion. 'But when we are judged', he goes on, 'we are chastened of the Lord, that we may not be condemned with the world' (verse 32). Sufferings of various kinds that the Christian may meet are not to be regarded as nameless evils. Rather they are tokens of God's love. They are the indication that His fatherly hand is over us, and that He will not let us continue in some sinful way without 'judging' us, so that we may return to our rightful allegiance.[1] Similarly the writer to the Hebrews reminds us that 'whom the Lord loveth he chasteneth, and scourgeth every son whom he receiveth' (Heb. xii. 6). He goes on to say that chastening 'yieldeth peaceable fruit unto them that have been exercised thereby, even the fruit of righteousness' (verse 11). The terminology is not the same as that in 1 Corinthians, but the thought is similar.

Again, Paul thanks God 'for your patience and faith in all your persecutions and in the afflictions which ye endure; which is a manifest token of the righteous judgement of God' (2 Thes. i. 4f.). We would not normally regard persecutions and afflictions as indications of God's righteous judgment, but two observations are in place. The one is that it is not the troubles themselves, but the bearing of the Thessalonian Christians in the troubles that seems to be the 'manifest token'. The other is that, as we saw in the previous paragraph, troubles and difficulties are part of the Lord's dealings with His people. He continually judges them, and leads them through the harsh things of this life to the glory that He has prepared for them. The difficulties the Christian meets are not to be regarded simply as cross accidents. They are the means God uses to discipline His people. They have the effect of bringing out qualities of Christian character that never emerge during the piping days of peace and ease.

But though God uses chastening to bring His people along the path of Christian development, we ought not to think that His judgments are arbitrary. They arise out of the nature of man's

---

[1] G. Vos comments on the judgment in this passage, 'this happens not to the detriment of their final salvation, rather to the furtherance of it' (*The Pauline Eschatology*, Grand Rapids, 1952, p. 270).

sin, and are related thereto. Abraham Lincoln brings out the point. 'Fondly do we hope—fervently do we pray—that this mighty scourge of war may speedily pass away. Yet, if God wills that it continue until all the wealth piled by the bondsman's two hundred and fifty years of unrequited toil shall be sunk, and until every drop of blood drawn with the lash shall be paid by another drawn with the sword, as was said three thousand years ago, so still it must be said, "The judgments of the Lord are true and righteous altogether".'[1] Here is the natural human shrinking from suffering. But it is coupled with the realization that life is a serious business in which the righteous judgments of God are worked out and must be worked out. There is also a readiness to accept the judgments of the Lord for what they are. Such an attitude alone can bring men profit as they go through deep waters.

Much 'corrective' punishment in modern times bears little relationship to the crime. Indeed, justice is admittedly not its basis. It is designed to correct, and it is allotted on that basis.[2] Many passages of Scripture remind us that God's judgments are righteous. 'Every transgression and disobedience received a just recompense of reward' (Heb. ii. 2). Peter reminds us that the Father 'without respect of persons judgeth according to each man's work' (I Pet. i. 17), and he can characterize Him as 'him that judgeth righteously' (I Pet. ii. 23). In the Revelation there is

[1] *Second Inaugural Address*. Yet this must not be elevated to an explanation of all the world's suffering. As G. Aulen reminds us, 'the conception of divine punishment cannot be employed as a rational explanation of the world's desolation and suffering' (*The Faith of the Christian Church*, London, 1954, p. 174). There are other causes for suffering. All that we are contending for is that there are occasions when God's chastening hand is to be discerned in the judgments which come upon men and nations.

[2] C. S. Lewis makes some incisive criticisms of the modern Humanitarian theory of punishment in an article published in *Twentieth Century*, vol. iii, no. 3 (and subsequently in *The Churchman*, vol. lxxiii, pp. 55 ff.). He argues that no theory which regards punishment as essentially deterrent or curative can be finally satisfactory, but only one which recognizes punishment as deserved. Norval Morris and Donald Buckle reply in *Twentieth Century*, vol. vi, no. 2, but they hardly touch the main point, being content to argue that the experts can be controlled, and that some element of deterrence and cure is inescapable. See also the discussion by L. Hodgson, *The Doctrine of the Atonement*, London, 1951, ch. III. Hodgson argues that punishment must be retributive and adds the point that it is not a private activity, but one exercised by a community towards its members.

exultation at the way the Lord God makes the punishment fit the crime: 'Righteous art thou, which art and which wast, thou Holy One, because thou didst thus judge: for they poured out the blood of saints and prophets, and blood hast thou given them to drink: they are worthy' (Rev. xvi. 5f.). Even the altar is moved to say, 'Yea, O Lord God, the Almighty, true and righteous are thy judgements' (verse 7). Perhaps the point is made most forcefully in the opening chapter of Romans with its reminder that God's wrath[1] is being revealed (Rom. i. 18) and its threefold 'God gave them up' (Rom. i. 24, 26, 28). Sin is even now reaping a terrible reward.

Two last points we make about the Father's present judgments. The one is in Revelation xviii. 8, 'strong is the Lord God which judged her'. Evil is strong in this world, and the forces of good so often seem pitiably inadequate. But there are times when appearances are deceptive. The Christian knows with an unshakeable certainty that God is over all, and 'strong is the Lord God which judgeth'. The other is seen in the parable in Luke xiii. 6-9. The owner of the fig tree, after three barren seasons, suggests cutting it down. 'Why doth it also cumber the ground?' But the vinedresser urges further delay. 'Let it alone this year also, till I shall dig about it, and dung it: and if it bear fruit thenceforth, well; but if not, thou shalt cut it down.' In other words there is nothing hasty about the judgments of the Lord. He exhausts every resource to bring about fruitfulness. Even when men say, 'There is no point in giving a further chance', He says, 'Let there be one more opportunity'. When the judgment of God falls upon a man he may be sure that he has exhausted the resources of the divine patience, and that these resources are not meagre.[2]

[1] Karl Barth comments, 'The wrath of God is the judgement under which we stand in so far as we do not love the Judge; it is the "No" which meets us when we do not affirm it; it is the protest pronounced always and everywhere against the course of the world in so far as we do not accept the protest as our own . . . The judgement under which we stand is a fact, quite apart from our attitude to it. Indeed it is the fact most characteristic of our life' (on Rom. i. 18).

[2] Joseph Conrad can say, in *The Life Beyond*, 'What humanity needs is not the promise of scientific immortality, but compassionate pity in this life and infinite mercy on the Day of Judgment'. The Bible makes it clear that that infinite mercy is extended.

III. THE JUDGMENT OF THE CHRIST

From the very beginning it was clear that Jesus' mission included a stern condemnation of evil. John the Baptist said that He would baptize 'with the Holy Ghost and with fire: whose fan is in his hand, and he will throughly cleanse his theshing-floor; and he will gather his wheat into the garner, but the chaff he will burn up with unquenchable fire' (Mt. iii. 11f.). Baptism with fire may well point to the fire of judgment,[1] the fire that purges out the dross, and it is certain that the rest of the saying conveys this thought. Christ's continual demand for repentance and His unsparing denunciation of evil wherever He found it shows how seriously the thought must be taken.

The demand for repentance brings us to another feature of judgment in the New Testament. It is primarily a judgment of individuals. In the Old Testament whole nations are frequently addressed, and judgment falls on them. In the New Testament, while social and communal responsibility is not overlooked, the emphasis in judgment is on what the individual does or does not do.

John has some interesting things to say about Christ's present activities as Judge of men. Of course, this does not differ essentially from the judgment of the Father, for the two are one. Jesus says, 'I can of myself do nothing: as I hear, I judge: and my judgement is righteous; because I seek not mine own will, but the will of him that sent me' (Jn. v. 30). And again, 'if I judge, my judgement is true; for I am not alone, but I and the Father that sent me' (Jn. viii. 16). The unity between the Father and the Son which is so strongly stressed in the Fourth Gospel means that the judgment passed by One is the judgment passed by the Other.[2]

But this Gospel is clear that the purpose of Jesus' coming was not judgment. 'For God sent not the Son into the world to judge

---

[1] W. H. Brownlee cites a passage from the Qumran Scrolls which 'makes it seem quite reasonable to suppose that the baptism of fire of which John spoke may have been in the torments of hell ... We would then interpret the baptism with the Spirit with reference to those who sincerely accepted John's baptism and reserve the baptism with fire for those who either refused or underwent hypocritically John's rite' (*The Scrolls and the New Testament*, ed. K. Stendahl, London, 1958, pp. 42, 43).

[2] Cf. Chrysostom, 'the sentence of Each is given from the same Mind' (Homilies on St. John, xxxix. 4).

the world; but that the world should be saved through him' (Jn. iii. 17). 'I came not to judge the world, but to save the world' (Jn. xii. 47). John consistently pictures Jesus as the Saviour. He was sent by the Father for the express purpose of saving men, and He pursues His path undeviatingly. It is true that He will come again for judgment. It is not John's purpose to describe this in detail—his theme is salvation. He notices it, and points out that the Father has given the Son authority to execute judgment. He reminds his readers that 'all that are in the tombs shall hear his voice, and shall come forth; they that have done good, unto the resurrection of life; and they that have done ill, unto the resurrection of judgement' (Jn. v. 28f.). He does not dwell on this truth, but he knows it is there. He concentrates on salvation.

Yet paradoxically he can report Jesus as saying, 'For judgement came I into this world' (Jn. ix. 39). There is no more than a surface contradiction with the sayings we have already noticed. It was as little the purpose of Jesus to judge men at His first coming as it is the purpose of the sun to cast shadows. But if the sun shines on a landscape shadows are inevitable. They are involved in the very fact that the sun shines. And when the Son of God comes into the world bringing salvation it is inevitable that He will judge men by that very fact. He came not to bring peace, but a sword (Mt. x. 34). There is a sifting process.[1] The offer of salvation is divisive.[2] It separates between those who respond to the gracious offer and those who do not. And this process goes on. As E. Stauffer reminds us, 'History is *krisis*, is separation of souls'.[3]

John has a very important passage in which he tells us how this judgment operates. 'This is the judgement', he says, 'that the

[1] C. J. Wright points out that the Latin *cribrum*, 'a sieve', comes from the same root as the Greek word for judgment (*Jesus the Revelation of God*, London, 1950, p. 163).

[2] 'Judgment is inherent in the response made to Jesus ... The cross is crucial to the problem of judgment for it separates the enemies of Jesus from the believers' (E. C. Colwell and E. L. Titus, *The Gospel of the Spirit*, New York, 1953, p. 171).

[3] *The Theology of the New Testament*, London, 1955, p. 42. Cf. also the dictum attributed to Schelling, 'the history of the world is the judgment of the world'.

JUDGMENT IN THE NEW TESTAMENT: A PRESENT REALITY 51

light is come into the world, and men loved the darkness rather than the light; for their works were evil' (Jn. iii. 19). 'Judgement' here is *krisis*, which denotes the process, not *krima*, which means the sentence. John is not saying, 'This is the sentence that God has decreed'. He is saying, 'This is the process. Here is how it works'. 'The light', Christ (Jn. viii. 12), has come into the world. Because of this men are forced into a decision.[1] And they are judged by their attitude to Him.[2] The tragedy of it is that when they come face to face with Him sinful men have nothing to do with Him. The incredible truth is that men prefer their darkness to His light. Their deeds are evil, and they turn from Him.[3]

The importance of this cannot be overstressed. Men today often reject the whole idea of judgment. They feel that it is not in keeping with the concept of God as a loving Father that He should judge men, and sentence them to hell. This objection overlooks entirely the way that judgment works. It is not that a tyrannical God looks down grimly on men and picks out certain with whom He will have nothing to do. God is love.[4] Men

[1] Commenting on Jn. iii. 18 R. H. Strachan says, 'If, as the Evangelist says in *v.* 16, God confronts us personally with His own love in the life and death and resurrection of Jesus, something more is required than intellectual deliberation. We are called to make a moral decision' (*The Fourth Gospel*, London, 1955, p. 140).

[2] G. R. Beasley-Murray cites W. G. Kümmel, 'the present is itself already an eschatological, final time of decision, because in *this* present the man Jesus has appeared; each man is compelled to a refusal or recognition of him, and by it he determines beforehand for himself his judgment at the Last Judgment' (*Jesus and the Future*, London, 1954, p. 224).

[3] Cf. C. H. Dodd, 'The purpose and intention of the coming of Christ are in no sense negative or destructive, but wholly positive and creative; but by an inevitable reaction the manifestation of the light brings into view the ultimate distinction between truth and falsehood, between good and evil. Hence it is κρίσις, discrimination. Men by their response to the manifestation of light declare themselves, and so pronounce their own "judgment"' (*op. cit.*, p. 210).

[4] Cf. C. J. Wright, 'The nature of God is Love. The purpose of His Love is that men may have Life. But His purpose does not operate by compulsion: it involves a Judgement—a judgement which is intrinsic to the Fatherly relation of God to His children. The universe is no magical universe. God compels no man to receive His gifts' (*op. cit.*, p. 135).

sentence themselves.[1] They choose darkness and refuse light.

> 'Still, as of old,
> Man by himself is priced.
> For thirty pieces Judas sold
> Himself, not Christ.'[2]

In one sense Judas did not really sell Christ. The Lord had come to earth expressly in order that He might go to the cross. If we can imagine such a thing, had Judas been faithful and true that would not have prevented the crucifixion. Jesus came to die. But if he did not sell Jesus how irrevocably Judas sold himself. And the price he set on himself was thirty pieces of silver!

And the process goes on. Here is a man who is determined to build up his business and make money. It involves giving time to the business which he ought to be giving to other things. It includes the use of practices which in his better moments he can only describe as shady. It means that bowing down to mammon which is incompatible with Christ.[3] He builds his business up. He makes his money. Never let it be said that God in harsh revenge for the man's success has shut him out of heaven. He has shut himself out. He set on his immortal soul the price of his business. And he proceeded to sell himself for that. 'This is the

---

[1] Karl Barth comments on 'God gave them up' in Rom. i. 24, 'The forgetting of the true God is already itself the breaking loose of His wrath against those who forget Him (i. 18). The enterprise of setting up the "No-God" is avenged by its success . . . Our conduct becomes governed precisely by what we desire. By a strict inevitability we reach the goal we have set before us . . . And, moreover, the uncleanness of their relation to God submerges their lives also in uncleanness. When God has been deprived of His glory, men are also deprived of theirs.' He concludes with the grim comment, 'They have wished to experience the known god of this world: well! they have experienced him'.

[2] Cited from C. J. Wright, *op. cit.*, p. 164.

[3] Adela Florence Cory Nicolson might say
> 'Men should be judged, not by their tint of skin,
> The Gods they serve . . .' (*Men Should be Judged*).

But the latter part of her words is false. The gods men choose to serve show what men are.

judgement, that ... men loved the darkness rather than the light.'[1]

The principle that greater privilege means greater responsibility and sorer judgment runs through the New Testament. In John ix. 41 the sin of the Pharisees depends on their claim to see (were they blind, they would have no sin). In John xv. 22-24 those who saw Christ's works and heard His words have no excuse: they have seen and hated both the Son and the Father. Paul obtained mercy because his sin of blasphemy and persecution was done 'ignorantly in unbelief' (1 Tim. i. 13). In 2 Peter ii. 20ff. it is seen as better never to have known the way of righteousness than to have known it and turned back from it. Through all such passages there runs this theme of judgment. If men choose the lower way when they could have the higher, then they sentence themselves.[2] There is no point in shutting our eyes to this grim reality.[3]

[1] Dorothy Sayers has this comment on Dante's portrait of Francesca da Rimini: 'All the good is there; the charm, the courtesy, the instant response to affection, the grateful eagerness to please; but also all the evil; the easy yielding, the inability to say No, the intense self-pity.' She quotes Charles Williams, 'the excuse reveals itself as precisely the sin ... the persistent parleying with the occasion of sin, the sweet prolonged laziness of love, is the first surrender of the soul to Hell—small but certain' (*The Comedy of Dante Alighieri*, Cantica I, Hell, translated by Dorothy L. Sayers, Penguin Books, 1955, pp. 102f.). The last three words are significant.

[2] 'The judgment is pronounced by the sinner himself and he inflicts inexorably his own sentence' (B. F. Westcott, *op. cit.*, p. 96).

[3] W. H. Rigg draws attention to another aspect of judgment in a quotation from Professor James, 'The drunken Rip Van Winkle in Jefferson's play excuses himself for every fresh dereliction by saying, "I won't count this time!" Well! he may not count it, and a kind heaven may not count it; but it is being counted none the less. Down among his nerve-cells and fibres the molecules are counting it, registering and storing it up to be used against him when the next temptation comes. Nothing we ever do is, in strict literalness, wiped out' (*The Fourth Gospel and Its Message for Today*, London, 1952, p. 90). This brings out the inevitability of judgment on the physical level. The New Testament is concerned with judgment on a deeper level. It stresses that men by their own action pass sentence on their souls.

CHAPTER IV

JUDGMENT IN THE NEW TESTAMENT: A FUTURE CERTAINTY

IF in one sense it is true that men judge themselves here and now by their reaction to Christ, the Light of the world, in another it is true that no judgment is final except that that God will dispense at the last day.[1] The New Testament has a very great deal to say on this subject, and we will select ten points in particular.

1. THE JUDGMENT IS AXIOMATIC

Men today often have difficulty with the idea of a day of judgment for the whole earth.[2] The mechanics of it trouble some, and the concept of God as a Judge bothers others.[3] Like the Greeks of

---

[1] But the one implies the other. Cf. E. Stauffer, 'The nearer the Church comes to the end of its history, the more destructive will persecutions and the final "offences" prove to be . . . Here the sifting of history reaches its climax, and there comes the revelation of the divine rejection, which is carried through in destruction' (*op. cit.*, p. 220).

[2] Theo Preiss finds it strange that final judgment 'figures so little in the theology and preaching of the Church. For many years, for example, Karl Barth has ceased to speak of it. Cullmann hardly mentions it. Niebuhr, like Barth of thirty years ago, seems to see only present judgment. There is certainly already a judgment implied in present events. The Magnificat proclaims that God abases the proud and exalts them of low degree. We should see in the storms of history the judgments of God foreshadowing the last judgment and in temporary deliverances the signs of the coming Kingdom. But there is also the last judgment which relativizes our poor human judgments and puts them in their place; it is above all our great consolation: one day the men and things of this world will be allocated to their true position, a new earth will at last know the meaning of justice' (*Life in Christ*, London, 1954, p. 79).

[3] E. A. Litton reminds us that we must not apply the analogy of human tribunals too literally. 'A human trial . . . is strictly a process of *investigation*' as a fallible judge and jury sift the evidence and try to get to the rights of the matter. In the last judgment 'The Judge is omniscient, and has no need of evidence to convince Him; He presides with a perfect knowledge of the character and history of every one who stands before Him . . . the great day will be one rather of *publication* and *execution* than of judgment strictly so called' (*Introduction to Dogmatic Theology*, London, 1960).

antiquity they reject the whole idea,[1] but the men of the New Testament were troubled by no such scruples. On the contrary, they held it to be fundamental and basic that God will judge all men.[2] If God be God, He must judge all creation.[3] Writing to the Romans Paul asks, 'But if our unrighteousness commendeth the righteousness of God, what shall we say? Is God unrighteous who visiteth with wrath?' He inserts a parenthesis to explain his bold language, 'I speak after the manner of men', and then proceeds, 'God forbid: for then how shall God judge the world?' (Rom. iii. 5f.). The final judgment is not something that must be argued for. It is something that may be argued from. Paul assumes that there will be no dispute about this. It is common ground for all Christians.[4] The writer to the Hebrews takes up much the same position when he speaks of 'eternal judgement' as one of 'the first principles of Christ' (Heb. vi. 1f.). Again Paul can make this final judgment the basis of an exhortation to his converts not to be harsh in their estimates of other people. It matters little, he says, that you should pass judgment on me,

---

[1] 'Greek thought had no room for such an eschatological judgment as the Biblical revelation announces' (F. F. Bruce, on Acts xvii. 31, *New International Commentary on the New Testament*).

[2] 'The idea of this final judgment is an essential, inalienable, and fundamental aspect of the outlook of faith' (G. Aulen, *op. cit.*, p. 176). He adds, 'But this does not mean that faith is able to answer all the questions which can be asked in this connection.'

[3] Cf. W. N. Clarke, 'God's judgment is not an arbitrary thing, or an act that is optional with the Judge . . . Only by abrogating his own moral order could God dispense with it' (*An Outline of Christian Theology*, Edinburgh, 1904, p. 460).

[4] It may be held to be a necessary deduction from the doctrine of monotheism. Paul writes to the Thessalonians, 'ye turned unto God from idols, to serve a living and true God, and to wait for his Son from heaven, whom he raised from the dead, even Jesus, which delivereth us from the wrath to come' (1 Thes. i. 9f.). Bultmann sees this passage as attesting 'the inter-relatedness of monotheistic and eschatological preaching' (*Theology of the New Testament*, vol. i, London, 1952, p. 74). James Denney says, 'It is not ethical to suppose that the moral condition of the world is that of an endless suspense, in which the good and the evil permanently balance each other, and contest with each other the right to inherit the earth' (*Studies in Theology*, London, 1895, p. 240).

or, for that matter, that any human tribunal[1] should do so. I do not even judge myself, he adds. He knows of nothing that would condemn him in the sight of God, but he is not justified by that. 'He that judgeth me is the Lord. Wherefore judge nothing before the time, until the Lord come' (1 Cor. iv. 3-5). That is to say, judging one another or even judging oneself is completely futile. There is one judgment that matters, and that is not here yet. Let us wait until the Lord come with His perfect judgment.

The certainty of judgment is deducible from the fact that Jesus unquestionably thought of Himself as the Messiah. He did not understand Messiahship in the same way as did the Jews of His day, but He knew that He was the Anointed One. It appears to have been universally held by those who looked for the Messiah that His coming would usher in a period of judgment and tribulation which they called 'the woes of the Messiah'. That Jesus did not repudiate this view is abundantly clear from His teaching on the second advent and the judgment He would then accomplish (Mt. xxv. 31ff.; Jn. v. 22, 27ff.). Messiahship does not exclude but rather implies judgment.

C. F. D. Moule has pointed out that both the sacraments imply a doctrine of judgment.[2] Baptism is regarded as dying with Christ and rising with Him. It is thus 'a willing acceptance of the verdict on sin, in union with Christ, whose perfect obedience to the sentence has been vindicated and crowned by the resurrection'.[3] Baptism 'is essentially pleading guilty, accepting the verdict'.[4] It is unrepeatable, and has about it the once-for-all quality of the final judgment. Holy Communion should be preceded by self-judgment, otherwise it will be followed by the

---

[1] 'Man's judgement' (1 Cor. iv. 3) is literally 'human day'. It is a very unusual expression, being found elsewhere only on an amulet of the second or third century. But the meaning does not seem to be in doubt.

[2] 'The Judgment Theme in the Sacraments' in *The Background of the New Testament and its Eschatology*, ed. W. D. Davies and D. Daube, Cambridge, 1956, pp. 464-481.

[3] *Op. cit.*, p. 466. T. W. Manson argues that Christian baptism is a development of that of John, and that his baptism is related to his preaching on judgment. Thus he sees Christian baptism in the light of the coming judgment (*Christian Worship*, ed. N. Micklem, Oxford, 1938, pp. 42ff.).

[4] *Op. cit.*, p. 467.

JUDGMENT IN THE NEW TESTAMENT: A FUTURE CERTAINTY 57

divine judgment (1 Cor. xi. 28f.). 'Emphatically, therefore, the Eucharist is an occasion of judgment—either of voluntary self-judgment, in acceptance of God's verdict on fallen man, or else of unwilling liability to God's judgment.'[1]

In modern writings the tendency is to minimize or overlook this strand of Scriptural teaching. For example, C. H. Dodd's 'realized eschatology' puts all the emphasis on the present. For him 'The *eschaton* has moved from the future to the present, from the sphere of expectation into that of realised experience'.[2] 'It is surely clear that, for the New Testament writers in general, the *eschaton* has entered history; the hidden rule of God has been revealed; the Age to Come has come.'[3] When he speaks of judgment, though he notices that Paul, for example, spoke of a final judgment,[4] Dodd puts all his emphasis on the present. 'God is confronting (men) in His kingdom, power and glory. This world has become the scene of a divine drama. It is the hour of decision. It is realised eschatology.'[5] 'Yet the Kingdom of God does come with judgment. The religious leaders, who censured Jesus for His work and teaching, were at that very moment pronouncing judgment upon themselves by the attitude they displayed, by their self-centred caution, their exclusiveness, their neglect of responsibilities, and their blindness to the purpose of God.'[6] 'An absolute end to history, whether it be conceived as coming soon or late, is no more than a fiction designed to express the reality of teleology within history.'[7] The last sentence in his

[1] *Op. cit.*, p. 472.
[2] *The Parables of the Kingdom*, London, 1938, p. 51.
[3] *The Apostolic Preaching and its Developments*, London, 1944, p. 85.
[4] 'We might fairly have inferred that there was in Paul's mind a fixed association of ideas—resurrection, lordship, judgment—even if he had not explicitly stated that in his preaching of the gospel he proclaimed a "day when God judges the secrets of men through Christ Jesus" (Rom. ii. 16)' (*Apostolic Preaching*, p. 12).
[5] *Parables*, p. 198.
[6] *Op. cit.*, p. 290. Cf. also 'Once in the course of the ages the spirit of man was confronted, within history, with the eternal God in His kingdom, power and glory, and that in a final and absolute sense, there was a great encounter, a challenge and response, a death and resurrection; and divine judgment and life eternal came into human experience' (*The Apostolic Preaching*, p. 75).
[7] *The Apostolic Preaching*, p. 82.

book, *The Apostolic Preaching*, thinks of the Last Judgment as no more than 'the least inadequate myth of the goal of history'.[1]

As we insisted in an earlier section, the New Testament does lay emphasis on the idea of a present judgment. But to say that it bears witness to no other judgment is palpably false. Statements about the future judgment are so frequent, and so basic to the thought of the biblical writers, that no theology which fails to do justice to it can be reckoned as true to the New Testament faith. 'If in this life only we have hoped in Christ, we are of all men most pitiable', wrote Paul (1 Cor. xv. 19). Hope is one of the great key thoughts of the New Testament, and this hope is centred on Him who once died for men, and who will return to be their Judge, and to set up the Kingdom in all its fulness.[2] A purely 'realized' eschatology is calamitous alike in its failure to reckon with the message of the New Testament,[3] and in its tragic consequences.[4]

[1] *Op. cit.*, p. 96.
[2] O. Cullmann says, 'Just as the "Victory Day" does in fact present *something new* in contrast to the decisive battle already fought at some point or other of the war, just so the end which is still to come also brings something new ... The new thing that the "Victory Day" brings, in addition to the decision already reached, is that the Holy Spirit, the πνεῦμα, lays hold of the entire world of the flesh (σάρξ), of matter' (*Christ and Time*, London, 1951, p. 141). The adequacy of Cullmann's view of the 'new thing' is open to debate, but his other point is valuable. D-day may mean that V-day is inevitable, but it is not itself V-day. The cross means that the decisive battle is won, the final victory is inevitable. But it does not mean that there will be no *parousia* and judgment.
[3] Neil Q. Hamilton says, 'Realized eschatology seeks ... to exhaust divine judgment in historical consequences of sinfulness'. He quotes from Dodd, 'The divine judgment is not a bare sentence, or expression of opinion. It is historical action', and proceeds, 'In criticism it must be said that with Paul, also, the judgment of God is no mere expression of opinion. But according to Rom. 2 the execution of that judgment is reserved for the *future* as an expression of God's wrath, and is not fulfilled in the ordinary events of history' (*The Holy Spirit and Eschatology in Paul*, Edinburgh and London, 1957, p. 66). That is the point to which we keep coming back. Realized eschatology picks those Scriptures which suit it, and ignores or explains away those which do not.
[4] J. E. Fison complains that to ignore the *parousia* as Dodd does 'is to do less than justice to the essential faith of the New Testament and to cut the nerve of the theological virtue of hope which is in such sorely short supply among us in consequence' (*op. cit.*, p. 63). He goes on to speak of 'the fatal legacy' left by realized eschatology.

The objections raised against Dodd's realized eschatology apply also to R. Bultmann's 'reinterpreted eschatology'. Bultmann repeatedly stresses the view that judgment is no more than a present activity. 'The historicizing of eschatology already introduced by Paul is radically carried through by John . . . The judgment takes place in just the fact that upon the encounter with Jesus the sunderance between faith and unfaith, between the sighted and the blind, is accomplished . . . The judgment, then, is no dramatic cosmic event, but takes place in the response of men to the word of Jesus.'[1] But to make his point he has to resort to a good deal of critical surgery. For example, he regards 'on the last day' as 'a later ecclesiastical redaction' in John vi. 39, 40, 44, xii. 48. Similarly he excises John vi. 51b-58, v. 28f., etc. Such a procedure gives us a good deal of information about the ideas of Bultmann, but little about New Testament teaching.[2]

II. JUDGMENT-DAY WILL BE MAJESTIC

When the Lord was on earth it was possible for men to pass Him by. Now that He is gone back to heaven it is possible for men to ignore Him, even deny His very existence. But when He comes again to judge it will be in such majesty that there will be no possibility of mistaking the grandeur of His person. He will come 'with ten thousands of his holy ones, to execute judgement upon all . . .' (Jude 14f.). He will come 'with the angels of his power in flaming fire (i.e. flaming fire is the robe of the majestic Judge), rendering vengeance to them that know not God, and to them that obey not the gospel of our Lord Jesus' (2 Thes. i. 7f.). At that day 'the heavens shall pass away with a great noise, and the elements shall be dissolved with fervent heat, and the earth and

---

[1] *Theology of the New Testament*, vol. ii, p. 38. Similarly Franz Kafka says, 'Only our concept of Time makes it possible for us to speak of the Day of Judgment by that name; in reality it is a summary court in perpetual session' (*Letters*).

[2] Neil Q. Hamilton says that Bultmann reduces 'time, the eschatological age to come and the Spirit which is the agent of that age, to merely subjective experiences of "the man of faith"'. He adds, 'There would be no criticism of such a programme if the declared intention were to depart from Pauline thought as a norm for such a theology and on the basis of certain other presuppositions create a new theology. But to profess to exhibit in such a theology the "real intention" of Paul is claiming too much' (*op. cit.*, p. 81).

the works that are therein shall be burned up' (2 Pet. iii. 10). Revelation describes a 'great white throne, and him that sat upon it, from whose face the earth and the heaven fled away'. The dead, 'the great and the small', stood before the throne and were judged out of the books, according to their works (Rev. xx. 11f.). Paul knows of a day when all men will appear before Christ's judgment-seat (2 Cor. v. 10; cf. Rom. xiv. 10). Our Lord Himself spoke of coming 'in his glory, and all the angels with him', of sitting 'on the throne of his glory', of having 'all the nations' gathered before Him. Then 'he shall separate them one from another, as the shepherd separateth the sheep from the goats'. He will send one group 'into eternal punishment' and the other 'into eternal life' (Mt. xxv. 31-46). Just how much of all this is the language of symbol we are not able to say. But what is clear is that the Judge is understood as a regal personage, as One whose appearance is awe-ful beyond description, as dispensing final justice with a royal hand. This great day is everywhere assumed throughout the New Testament. There are preliminary judgments of God throughout history. But at the end there will be the climax, that which proceeds out of the preliminary and partial judgments, and which perfectly fulfils all that they foreshadow.[1]

A variety of ways of referring to the Day is found. It is called 'the day of God' (2 Pet. iii. 12), 'the day of the Lord' (2 Pet. iii. 10), 'the day of the Lord Jesus' (1 Cor. v. 5), 'the day of our Lord Jesus Christ' (1 Cor. i. 8), 'the day of Christ' (Phil. ii. 16), 'that day' (2 Thes. i. 10), 'the last day' (Jn. vi. 39), 'the great day' (Jude 6), 'the day of wrath and revelation of the righteous judgement of God' (Rom. ii. 5), 'the day of redemption' (Eph. iv. 30), 'the day of visitation' (1 Pet. ii. 12), 'the great day of their wrath' (Rev. vi. 17), 'the great day of God, the Almighty' (Rev.

---

[1] P. T. Forsyth reminds us that, 'For the Bible as a whole, whether rising to the Cross or spreading from it, history is viewed under the category of judgment (though saving judgment) and not under that of progress. Eschatology goes much deeper than evolution . . . The course of historic events is that of a series of judgments . . . a long crescendo of judgment, ending in a crisis of all the crises, a harvest of all the harvests which had closed one age and begun a new, a grand climacteric of judgment, a last judgment, which dissipates for ever in a storm the silting up of all previous judgments, because ending a temporal world and opening an eternal' (*The Justification of God*, London, 1916, p. 185).

xvi. 14), 'the day of judgement' (1 Jn. iv. 17). This multiplicity of ways of referring to the day indicates something of the fascination it had for the men of the New Testament and also something of its many-sided grandeur.

III. CHRIST THE JUDGE

The Father judges all men, but He does not do this in person. 'He hath given all judgement unto the Son' (Jn. v. 22).[1] This is particularly the case in respect of the final judgment. In the judgment scene in Matthew xxv. 31-46 the Son of man is the judge.[2] Peter tells us that 'this is he which is ordained of God to be the Judge of quick and dead' (Acts x. 42). Paul speaks of 'the crown of righteousness, which the Lord, the righteous judge, shall give to me at that day' (2 Tim. iv. 8). This truth is so basic that it has been caught up into the creeds of the Church: 'he shall come again with glory to judge both the quick and the dead', 'from thence he shall come to judge the quick and the dead'.

Throughout the New Testament Jesus appears as our Saviour. He came to earth expressly to put away our sins, which meant dying on the cross. This is our assurance that the final judgment

---

[1] J. E. Fison sees in this the distinctive New Testament teaching on the subject. 'The new element in New Testament eschatology is not bound up with the fact of judgment, however, but with the person of the judge ... The judgment which his incarnation necessarily involved was the inevitable corollary of the grace and blessedness which he came to bestow' (*op. cit.*, p. 133).

[2] T. W. Manson takes 'the Son of Man' as 'a name for Jesus plus any who take up the cross and follow him' (*The Teaching of Jesus*, Cambridge, 1939, p. 269). He understands the judgment in this light, 'The "Son of Man" is a corporate body and the rest of mankind are judged by their treatment of that body in the days of their power and its weakness' (*op. cit.*, p. 270). It seems better, however, to understand judgment as exercised by Christ Himself. While the criterion in this passage is admittedly the way men have reacted towards Christ's people, yet Jesus is not describing the activity of a group, but of a person, and that person Himself. S. Mowinckel finds in Judaism a distinction between the Messiah and the Son of Man, while agreeing that each concept was affected by the other. He denies that the Messiah was thought of as judge of men (*op. cit.*, pp. 313, 319, 336, etc.), but has an important section in which he emphasizes that in apocalyptic circles it was held that God would exercise the final judgment through the Son of Man (*op cit.*, pp. 393ff.).

will be a judgment of love.[1] But it does not mean that judgment ceases to be a grim reality. The self-sacrificing love we see on Calvary is in itself the most damning judgment imaginable on the self-seeking life. Jesus Himself, immediately after saying 'I came not to judge the world, but to save the world', went on 'He that rejecteth me, and receiveth not my sayings, hath one that judgeth him: the word that I spake, the same shall judge him in the last day' (Jn. xii. 47f.). Though Jesus came with words of comfort and salvation, yet the man who turns away from them will find them words of condemnation at the last day. This is the reflex side of salvation. James tells us that we are to be judged 'by a law of liberty' (Jas. ii. 12). The very freedom that we have will condemn us if we fail to use it rightly.[2]

IV. ALL MEN WILL BE JUDGED

The judgment will be such that none may escape it.[3] The living and the dead are involved (2 Tim. iv. 1; 1 Pet. iv. 5). Even angels are included (2 Pet. ii. 4; Jude 6). God is 'the Judge of all' (Heb. xii. 23). It is the temptation of religious man to think that he will escape in such a time. He can understand such a saying as 'fornicators and adulterers God will judge' (Heb. xiii. 4). He can appreciate the force of Paul's dictum that all will be judged 'who

---

[1] Cf. G. Aulen, 'This in itself is the strongest possible expression of the fact that Christian faith cannot conceive of God's judgment in any other terms than as a judgment of love itself, and that no assertion about God's judgment can be identified as Christian which cannot also be ascribed to and affirmed of Christ and the Holy Spirit' (*op. cit.*, p. 170).

[2] Cf. J. E. Fison, 'The importance of realizing that Jesus Christ is the judge cannot be overemphasized. At the end we shall not approach a distant doomsday, but we shall be confronted by an immediate presence. If only we realized it, it is the presence of a living and loving person, however mediated, with whom we have to deal here and now, and with whom we are bound to deal hereafter' (*op. cit.*, pp. 48f.). James Denney sees in the thought of Christ as judge both hope and solemnity. 'The Christian hope is not clouded by the judgment-seat of Christ; it is sustained at the holy height which befits it' (*The Second Epistle to the Corinthians* (The Expositor's Bible, London, 1907, p. 184)).

[3] Rudyard Kipling reminds us that earthly distinctions vanish away before this dread reality.
'Oh, East is East, and West is West, and never the twain shall meet,
Till Earth and Sky stand presently at God's great Judgment Seat'
(*The Ballad of East and West*). But they do meet in the judgment.

believed not the truth, but had pleasure in unrighteousness' (2 Thes. ii. 12). But he likes to think of himself as immune. It is this attitude of which T. F. Torrance complains in the medieval church. 'Here the *Eschaton* is so domesticated and housed within the Church that, far from standing under final judgment, the Church dispenses it by her binding and loosing, far from being repentant and reformable, the Church can only develop according to her own immanent norms which correspond to the fixed pattern of the Kingdom.'[1]

But the New Testament will not leave religious man to rest in his complacent smugness. It prods him wide awake with its insistence that he, too, stands under judgment. Take the saying quoted in Hebrews x. 30 (Dt. xxxii. 36), 'The Lord shall judge his people'. This brings the matter unpleasantly close to home. And it is even worse with 1 Peter iv. 17, 'the time is come for judgement to begin at the house of God'. Jesus assures us that people like the scribes, with religious pretensions, 'shall receive greater condemnation' (Mk. xii. 40), and James reminds us that Christian teachers 'shall receive heavier judgement' (Jas. iii. 1) Jesus tells us that in the judgment some will say, 'Lord, Lord, did we not prophesy by thy name, and by thy name cast out devils, and by thy name do many mighty works?' only to receive His sentence, 'I never knew you: depart from me, ye that work iniquity' (Mt. vii. 22f.). Those with special privileges will be judged the more severely. As J. V. Langmead Casserley expresses it, 'They that take the gospel to themselves must either live by the glory of the gospel or perish beneath the judgment of the gospel'.[2] So far from getting off lightly in the judgment, religious man will find himself judged more strictly, precisely on account of

---

[1] *Kingdom and Church*, Edinburgh and London, 1956, p. 2. The same essential position seems implied in the criticism of the Evanston Report by the Eastern Orthodox delegation that it insufficiently recognized that 'the Church of Christ, as the realized Kingdom of God, lies beyond Judgment' (cited in W. M. Horton, *Christian Theology*, London, 1956, p. 260; Horton nevertheless thinks them 95 per cent in agreement with the Report). Contrast Calvin, 'Whenever believers meet in one place, in the name of Christ, there is already in their assembly a sort of image of the future judgment, which will be perfectly brought to light on the last day' (Torrance, *op. cit.*, p. 139).

[2] *Op. cit.*, pp. 76f.

his greater privileges.¹ To ignore this is to overlook a truth which the New Testament reiterates again and again. It is worth noting that the people who will be surprised on that day are not the rank outsiders, but those who think themselves safe within the church.²

V. ALL THINGS WILL BE JUDGED

The judgment of which Scripture speaks is one in which nothing can be kept hid. 'God shall judge the secrets of men' (Rom. ii. 16). The Lord 'will both bring to light the hidden things of darkness, and make manifest the counsels of the hearts' (1 Cor. iv. 5; cf. Mk. iv. 22; Lk. xii. 2f.). Most of us could face the judgment calmly if we could be assured that certain things would remain hidden. But *all* our deeds stand under judgment, and there's the rub. 'All' includes all the little evil deeds, as well as the big ones. 'Every idle word that men shall speak, they shall give account thereof in the day of judgement' (Mt. xii. 36). It is the far-reaching and all-inclusive nature of the judgment that makes it so frightening. At the same time, the thought that all we do matters in God's sight helps make life worth living. It gives a dignity to even the most insignificant action, the most unimportant word.³ Even the giving of a cup of cold water will not go unnoticed.⁴ We should also bear in mind that Paul adds to the

---

¹ Cf. L. Berkhof, 'The standard by which saints and sinners are judged will evidently be the revealed will of God. This is not the same for all. Some have been privileged above others, and this naturally adds to their responsibility' (*Systematic Theology*, Grand Rapids, 1946, p. 733).

² Cf. J. E. Fison, 'as so often ecclesiastically proclaimed, the one thing that the last judgment is never allowed to do is the one thing that in the New Testament it is most designed to do. Its purpose there is to spring a complete surprise not upon the lost pagan souls outside the pale of the church, but upon the complacent ecclesiastical souls whose entire confidence is based upon the fact that they are well within it' (*op. cit.*, p. 249).

³ Cf. James Denney, 'we cannot afford to have life, even at its lowest, robbed of the awfulness, the grandeur, the absolute moral worth which it thus obtains' (*Studies in Theology*, London, 1895, p. 244). P. T. Forsyth points out that apathy about final judgment 'works out into a disbelief of judgment radical and ubiquitous, into a light sense of spiritual wickedness in high places, and into the moral cynicism and cruelty of the natural man as statesman or man of the world' (*op. cit.*, p. 200).

⁴ 'The gift of a cup of cold water is just about the absolute minimum; but even the minimum counts . . . A gift, even the smallest, in the name of Jesus is essentially a gift for the advancement of his cause, the cause of God and

[*Continued on next page.*]

words about judgment quoted above from Romans ii. 16, 'according to my gospel'. Judgment is not some horrible disaster to be set over against the gospel. It is the outworking of the essential message of the gospel. That all of life is sufficiently important for God to take notice of it and to require account of it is not something to be repudiated and shunned. It is to be welcomed. It is part of the good news.

VI. THE JUDGMENT IS INESCAPABLE

'It is appointed unto men once to die, and after this—judgement' (Heb. ix. 27; there is nothing in the Greek to correspond to the 'cometh' of RV). Judgment is as inescapable as death. Indeed, it is more so, for the New Testament envisages that some will still be alive at the second coming, and thus will not see death, but it does not envisage any as escaping judgment. For some there is 'a certain fearful expectation of judgement' (Heb. x. 27), but fearful or not men may not escape it. Paul asks a rhetorical question, 'reckonest thou this, O man . . . that thou shalt escape the judgement of God' (Rom. ii. 3; cf. Mt. xxiii. 33). And the answer is never in doubt. Basically the idea goes back to Jesus Himself. As J. Jeremias puts it, 'The message of Jesus is not only the proclamation of salvation, but also the announcement of judgement, a cry of warning, and a call to repentance in view of the terrible urgency of the crisis. The number of parables in this category is nothing less than awe-inspiring'.[1] The call for repentance and the note of urgency runs right through the Gospels.

This aspect of Jesus' teaching is unpalatable to modern man. So he simply rejects it. He has largely dismissed the thought of final judgment from his mind. He does not think of himself as accountable. The New Testament does not share his unreasoning

---

God's righteousness, in the world: and such a gift is presumptive evidence that the heart of the giver is in the right place' (T. W. Manson, *op. cit.*, pp. 271f.).

[1] *The Parables of Jesus*, London, 1954, p. 120. He further says concerning the 'judgment' parables, 'It is not their purpose to propound moral precepts, but to shock into realization of its danger a nation rushing upon its own destruction, and more especially its leaders, the theologians and priests. But above all they are a call to repentance' (*op cit.*, p. 126).

optimism.¹ It insists that over and above the judgment which inevitably falls on man here and now there is a final judgment when all men will stand before the tribunal of God. The judgment there dispensed has the character of finality which none of the partial and anticipatory judgments of this earth can share.²

VII. JUDGMENT IS ACCORDING TO WORKS

It is the consistent teaching of the New Testament that judgment will be according to works (Mt. xvi. 27; Rom. ii. 6; 1 Cor. iii. 8; Rev. xxii. 12; etc.). The principle is worked out in Matthew xxv. 31-46. The Son of man says to those who are to inherit the kingdom, 'I was an hungred, and ye gave me meat: I was thirsty, and ye gave me drink: I was a stranger, and ye took me in; naked, and ye clothed me: I was sick, and ye visited me: I was in prison, and ye came unto me.' All this is explained in the words, 'Inasmuch as ye did it unto one of these my brethren, even these least, ye did it unto me.' A similar explanation is given of the fate of those who go away 'into eternal punishment'. In similar fashion, though without the concrete examples, Paul shows how judgment will work in Romans ii. 5-16. In this respect it is worth pointing out that from 1 Corinthians iii. 8 we learn that every man 'shall receive his own reward according to his own labour'. It is his 'labour', not his results that are the criterion. Judgment according to works means more to God than it can ever do with us, because He knows as we cannot the many factors which lie behind apparent success and failure.

There are some who object to the whole idea of eternal rewards,

[1] A. M. Hunter surveys the teaching of Jesus on judgment and then says, 'In all these matters of judgement to come Jesus spoke with reserve, not elaborating the picture (as many of His followers have done) but emphasising men's accountability to God and using the idea of doomsday to persuade men that eternal issues hung upon their response to the Reign of God decisively manifested in His person and mission' (*The Work and Words of Jesus*, London, 1956, p. 106).

[2] Reinhold Niebuhr speaks of 'the necessity . . . of a *final* judgment upon good and evil'. He also says, 'The idea of a "last" judgment expresses Christianity's refutation of all conceptions of history, according to which it is its own redeemer and is able by its process of growth and development, to emancipate man from the guilt and sin of his existence, and to free him from judgment' (*The Nature and Destiny of Man*, vol. ii, London, 1944, pp. 302, 303).

affirming that it is not true Christian service if we serve simply for reward. This affirmation may unhesitatingly be endorsed. Selfishness is not less selfishness because it is directed towards spiritual rather than material ends. If we serve for reward then that in itself indicates that we have not begun to understand the Christian way, and that there awaits us only condemnation. But that does not mean that God is to put all men on a flat level in the hereafter. Here and now the man who gives himself wholeheartedly to the service of Christ knows more of the joy of the Lord than the half-hearted. We have no warrant from the New Testament for thinking that it will be otherwise in heaven.[1]

There is a difficulty in that salvation is always regarded as due to the good gift of Christ, whereas judgment is invariably on the basis of works.[2] Such a passage as 1 Corinthians iii. 10-15 seems to give the reconciliation. 'Other foundation can no man lay than that which is laid, which is Jesus Christ.' That is to say, salvation comes only from what Christ has done. But men must live out their Christian lives and this is likened to a process of building: 'But if any man buildeth on the foundation gold, silver, costly stones, wood, hay, stubble . . .' That is to say, some men build carelessly. Their service of Christ is shoddy and half-hearted. Others build with care, putting their very best into all of life, regarded now as the living out of the faith. And, says Paul, 'the day shall declare it, because it is revealed in fire; and the fire itself shall prove each man's work of what sort it is. If any man's work shall abide which he built thereon, he shall receive a reward. If any man's work shall be burned, he shall suffer loss: but he himself shall be saved; yet so as through fire'.[3]

---

[1] T. C. Hammond says that for believers, 'The judgment is chiefly in the nature of rewards for stewardship'. He goes on to say, 'Sin voluntarily permitted to remain in habitual operation in the life of the Christian cannot but cause his serious loss at the judgment seat. The Christian is never given any encouragement for antinomianism' (*In Understanding Be Men*, London, 1936, p. 245).

[2] Cf. Alan Richardson, 'This doctrine of a judgment of Christians according to their works is no mere relic of Paul's Pharisaic ideology; it is no unconscious clinging to a doctrine of works. It is an assertion of the seriousness of the moral struggle in the Christian life' (*An Introduction to the Theology of the New Testament*, London, 1955, p. 342).

[3] Cf. J. Burnier, 'A life inspired by love ought to manifest the reality of our justification by Jesus Christ. Thus the idea of a justification according to

[*Continued on next page.*]

VIII. THE JUDGMENT IS JUST

If all men are to be judged, and if judgment is to be on the basis of works then we need above all to know that the judgment will be perfectly just.[1] We might be left to infer this from the nature of God, but Scripture goes further. It specifically assures us that 'the judgement of God is according to truth' (Rom. ii. 2). Judgment is only without mercy 'to him that hath shewed no mercy' (Jas. ii. 13).[2] He that is called 'Faithful and True . . . in righteousness . . . doth judge' (Rev. xix. 11).

But we must not think of this perfect justice as a strict and bare legalism. As in the Old Testament, with God's justice there is mingled mercy. There is one consistent attitude.[3] We must not think of God's mercy pulling Him in one direction and His justice in another. He acts in accordance with His consistent purpose. And this purpose is one of merciful justice. 'Judgement and the love of God' are closely linked (Lk. xi. 42). When James says that 'mercy glorieth against judgement' (Jas. ii. 13) he is not

---

works does not contradict the doctrine of justification by faith. On the contrary, the latter implies the former' (von Allmen, *op. cit.*, p. 214). Cf. also Emil Brunner, 'At the day of divine judgment actions are decisive. This does not stand in opposition to the doctrine of grace and faith . . . but is, on the contrary, at one with it. The question is not whether the doing of good is decisive, but whether one arrives at the doing of good in his own strength' (*The Letter to the Romans*, London, 1959, p. 20).

[1] A. A. Hodge goes into detail. 'The judgment will not rest upon appearances, nor testimony, nor any partial knowledge of the facts, nor upon technical grounds of law, nor specific actions dissociated from the state of the heart and the motives which prompted them' (*The Confession of Faith*, 1958, p. 393).

[2] Nicholas Berdyaev seems totally to ignore this line of Scriptural teaching. He says, for example, 'The justification of hell on the grounds of justice, such as we find it in St. Thomas Aquinas and Dante, is particularly revolting and lacking in spiritual depth' (*The Destiny of Man*, London, 1945, p. 267). But St. Thomas Aquinas and Dante are too great to be thus summarily dismissed. One feels that they were, at least, making a serious effort to face a problem that Berdyaev simply ignores. The God of the Bible is just. It is true that justice does not explain everything. It is true that the Bible says 'God is love' and it does not say 'God is justice'. But the justice of God is there. It is too facile altogether simply to overlook it.

[3] Cf. W. N. Clarke, 'It is a mistake to suppose that for the purpose of judgment God will assume some special sternness, or lay aside something of his essential grace. God never changes. Men will be judged by the same God who has created them, governed them, and sought to save them; for he is always the same (*op. cit.*, p. 462).

setting God's mercy and God's judgment in opposition. Rather he is affirming the importance of men's showing mercy in their dealings with one another. Only so will they escape condemnation.

IX. JUDGMENT IS SERIOUS

The New Testament leaves us in no doubt that the judgment that awaits us is one fraught with the most far-reaching consequences. Paul speaks of certain evil things in Romans i, and then says that it is 'the ordinance of God, that they which practise such things are worthy of death' (Rom. i. 32; cf. 'the wages of sin is death', vi. 23). Jesus spoke of some who would come forth out of the graves 'unto the resurrection of judgement' (which is set in contrast to 'the resurrection of life', Jn. v. 29). The writer to the Hebrews says that 'if we sin wilfully after that we have received the knowledge of the truth, there remaineth no more a sacrifice for sins, but a certain fearful expectation of judgement' (Heb. x. 26f.). While we may be sure that the mercy of God reaches as far as mercy can reach we should not be blind to the fact that in the final judgment serious issues are involved.[1] Sin must then be reckoned as sin and receive its just recompense.

To our generation this is practically incredible. It seems axiomatic to us that God in love will deliver all men. That is not what Scripture teaches. And, as a matter of fact, this view in the end loses what it seeks to protect. As McNeile Dixon reminds us, 'The kind-hearted humanitarians of the nineteenth century decided to improve on Christianity. The thought of Hell offended their susceptibilities. They closed it, and to their surprise the gates of Heaven closed also with a melancholy bang. The malignant countenance of Satan disturbed them. They dispensed with him and at the same time God took His departure'.[2] If we are to retain a fundamental Christian optimism we must insist on the serious issues involved in a real doctrine of judgment.

[1] O. C. Quick points out that 'Once the process of human response to God is complete, once its character in any human soul is finally fixed, there is no place left for anything but God's verdict. And the verdict is inevitable; it must be what it is. To talk of a merciful *verdict* is nonsense. The God of love cannot treat the ultimate rejection of love as though it were not rejection. Otherwise he would be as unloving as unrighteous' (*Doctrines of the Creed*, London, 1949, p. 253).

[2] Cited by F. J. Rae, *The Expository Times*, vol. lxvi, p. 215.

A further criticism of the view we are opposing is that it does not take seriously the meaning of love. As Aulen reminds us, 'the judgment of God is understood in the final analysis as an expression of his love. For the only really radical judgment of sin is that of pure love'.[1] Sin regarded as a breaking of the law of God is a serious matter. But when men turn away from the gift God proffers in Christ's redeeming love that is infinitely worse. The sin against love is the most heinous of all sins.[2] In the Bible the lot of the finally impenitent is the divine condemnation.

This is often expressed in the New Testament in terms of the wrath of God. This wrath is sometimes depicted as at work here and now (e.g. Rom. xiii. 4f.), but basically it is an eschatological concept. It is 'the wrath to come' (*hē mellousē orgē*, Mt. iii. 7; *hē orgē hē erchomenē*, 1 Thes. i. 10). In Romans ii the thoughts of the Day of Judgment and of the wrath to come interpenetrate. Indeed that Day is 'the day of wrath' (Rom. ii. 5). Attempts have been made to show that 'the wrath' is an impersonal process in the New Testament.[3] These attempts are in my judgment completely unsuccessful.[4] The God of the New Testament does not sit back and let 'natural' laws bring about the defeat of evil. He is actively opposed to evil in every shape and form. Where unpleasant consequences follow on evil-doing His hand is in it. In any case it is difficult to see what meaning can be attached to

---

[1] *Op. cit.*, p. 170. He also says, 'To be confronted by divine love involves always and everywhere a judgment. To stand before God is to be judged' (*op. cit.*, p. 172). Paul Tillich maintains that 'The ontological character of love solves the problem of the relation of love and retributive justice. Judgment is an act of love which surrenders that which resists love to self-destruction' (*Systematic Theology*, vol. i, London, 1955, p. 314).

[2] James Moffatt says, 'it is this revelation of love as the character of God the Father which involves the tremendous severity of judgment upon those who are guilty of the worst sin in the world—the sin against love' (*The Theology of the Gospels*, London, 1928, p. 120). He adds a footnote, 'On the Jewish scheme the judgment formed an essential part of the doctrine of the Law. When the latter was replaced or restated as love to God, implying love to one's neighbour, the conception of the divine judgment was correspondingly humanised and at the same time rendered more stringent'.

[3] Notably by C. H. Dodd, *Romans* (Moffatt N.T. Commentary), p. 23, etc.

[4] John Knox notices Dodd's argument and proceeds, 'But actually there is no way to eliminate the evidence that Paul also thought . . . of "the wrath" as the righteous judgment of God upon those who have disobeyed his will' (*The Death of Christ*, New York, 1958, p. 153).

an 'impersonal process' (as applied to moral affairs) in a universe where God is all-powerful and omnipresent. If God is a moral God He will certainly take vigorous action in opposition to evil. The wrath of God is a necessary consequence of His holiness,[1] His righteousness,[2] and His love.[3] With this must be taken the thought that the full weight of God's judgment and wrath has fallen on Christ (Rom. iii. 24ff.; 2 Cor. v. 21; 1 Jn. iv. 10).[4] It is precisely in the context of judgment that the atonement is to be understood. And if Christ bore such a heavy judgment 'how shall we escape, if we neglect so great salvation?' (Heb. ii. 3).

X. BELIEVERS MAY HAVE CONFIDENCE IN THE JUDGMENT

Though believers, like all the rest of mankind, face judgment they do not face it in the same way. The New Testament attitude is not one of coward shrinking from it, but of anticipation in mingled joy[5] and solemnity.[6] For in P. T. Forsyth's phrase, the judgment 'always means the dawn of the kingdom more than the doom of the world'.[7] 'Who shall lay anything to the charge of God's elect?' asks Paul. 'It is God that justifieth; who is he that shall condemn?' (Rom. viii. 33). 'God is not unrighteous to forget your work', says the writer to the Hebrews, 'and the love which ye

---

[1] Cf. Emil Brunner, 'the conception of judgment flows necessarily from a recognition of the holiness of God. God is He who takes His Will in absolute seriousness, He who is not mocked'. 'If there is no last judgment, it means that God does not take His own will seriously' (*Eternal Hope*, London, 1954, pp. 173, 179).

[2] Cf. A. Richardson, 'God's wrath is an inevitable consequence of his righteousness. The coming of Christ did not mean that God was no longer a God of wrath; on the contrary, it clearly revealed God's wrath against all human ungodliness and unrighteousness (Rom. i. 18)' (*op. cit.*, p. 76).

[3] The wrath of God is 'identical with the consuming fire of inexorable divine love in relation to our sins' (D. M. Baillie, *God Was in Christ*, London, 1955, p. 189).

[4] Cf. Richardson, 'The cross of Christ is the visible, historical manifestation of the ὀργὴ τοῦ Θεοῦ: it is the supreme revelation of the wrath of God, against all ungodliness and unrighteousness of men' (*op. cit.*, p. 77).

[5] J. E. Fison speaks of judgment as 'the reverse side of the thrilling joy and tingling hope with which the expectation of the end is again and again characterized by our Lord' (*op. cit.*, pp. 137f.; he goes on to remind us that the three abiding theological virtues include hope, not fear).

[6] Cf. G. Vos, 'While the judgment as such can not be otherwise regarded than as a matter of solemnity and fear, yet to this has now been added the reverse side, that of a prospect of joy and hopefulness' (*op. cit.*, p. 276).

[7] *Op. cit.*, p. 198.

shewed toward his name' (Heb. vi. 10). Jude's magnificent doxology looks to 'him that is able to guard you from stumbling, and to set you before the presence of his glory without blemish in exceeding joy' (Jude 24). And John speaks of love being 'made perfect with us, that we may have boldness in the day of judgement' (1 Jn. iv. 17). His word for 'boldness' is *parrhesia*, which literally means 'all speech'. It signifies the attitude when the words flow freely, when we feel quite at home. And Christians will feel at home on that great day, for it marks the triumph of their Saviour in the kingdom of their Father.[1] Why should they not feel at home as they see His will perfectly done?

The doctrine of final judgment enshrines many important truths. It stresses man's accountability and the certainty that justice will finally triumph over all the wrongs which are part and parcel of life here and now. The former gives a dignity to the humblest action, the latter brings calmness and assurance to those in the thick of the battle. This doctrine gives meaning to life. The Greek idea of history as a cyclic process shut men up to a treadmill in which they might strive mightily, but neither gods nor men could advance. The Christian view of judgment means that history moves to a goal. O. C. Quick refers to 'God's completing act in a fellowship of redeemed souls in a universe which is at once a new world and the perfection of the old'.[2] Judgment protects the idea of the triumph of God and of good. It is unthinkable that the present conflict between good and evil should last throughout eternity. Judgment means that evil will be disposed of authoritatively, decisively, finally. Judgment means that in the end God's will will be perfectly done.

[1] Karl Barth cites the Heidelberg Catechism, '"What comfort hast thou by the coming again of Christ to judge the quick and the dead?" Answer: "That in all my miseries and persecutions I look with my head erect for the very same, who before yielded Himself unto the judgment of God for me and took away all malediction from me, to come Judge from heaven. . . ." A different note is struck here. Jesus Christ's return to judge the quick and the dead is tidings of joy. "With head erect", the Christian, the Church may and ought to confront this future' (*Dogmatics in Outline*, London, 1949, p. 134).

[2] *Op. cit.*, p. 250. So also Westcott, 'In its universal aspect it (i.e. the Judgment) is the supreme declaration of the truth that there is an end, a goal for creation, a purpose to be fulfilled, a will to be accomplished' (*op. cit.*, p. 95).

www.ingramcontent.com/pod-product-compliance
Lightning Source LLC
Chambersburg PA
CBHW051706090426
42736CB00013B/2570